EXERCISES IN
ENGLISH
CONVERSATION

ROBERT J. DIXSON

EXERCISES IN

ENGLISH

CONVERSATION

A NEW REVISED EDITION

BOOK 2

PRENTICE HALL REGENTS, Englewood Cliffs, NJ 07632

Cover design: Paul Gamarello
Text design: Judy Allan, The Designing Woman
Illustrations: Steven Cavallo

 Published by Prentice Hall Regents
Prentice-Hall, Inc.
A Division of Simon & Schuster
Englewood Cliffs, New Jersey 07632

Printed in the United States of America

20   19   18   17   16   15   14   13

0-13-294679-3

Prentice-Hall International (UK) Limited, *London*
Prentice-Hall of Australia Pty. Limited, *Sydney*
Prentice-Hall Canada Inc., *Toronto*
Prentice-Hall Hispanoamericana, S.A., *Mexico*
Prentice-Hall of India Private Limited, *New Delhi*
Prentice-Hall of Japan, Inc., *Tokyo*
Simon & Schuster Asia Pte. Ltd., *Singapore*
Editora Prentice-Hall do Brasil, Ltda., *Rio de Janeiro*

Preface

This new, revised edition of *Exercises in English Conversation* Book 2 contains material for the high-intermediate and advanced student. The first volume, *Exercises in English Conversation* Book 1, offers material for the beginning and low-intermediate student.

Each unit is designed in the same pattern. First, a short, topical conversation or short story is followed by fifteen questions designed to test understanding and to stimulate conversation about the topic of the conversation or story. Next, a practice drill covers some specific point of grammar.

The drill, in turn, is followed by a ten-to-fifteen-question exercise providing practice in that point of grammar. Next, a vocabulary section allows for practice in all the new terminology of the lesson. Finally, a review section with fifteen questions covers topics and grammatical points introduced in previous lessons.

The grammar of *Exercises in English Conversation* (Books 1 and 2) follows, lesson for lesson, the grammar lessons of *Tests and Drills in English Grammar* (Books 1 and 2), the companion volumes to these books. For best results, *Tests and Drills in English Grammar* should be studied with these books.

In using *Exercises in English Conversation,* the teacher should keep the following suggestions in mind:

1. Require direct, complete, and automatic answers to all questions and all question-answer exercises throughout the books. If the students' answers are slow or hesitant, repeat the questions several times or demand more preparation at home.

2. Have students practice all answers at home many times—preferably aloud. Also, never work in class with material unpracticed by the students at home. Work, instead, for speed and automatism on familiar material. Five questions, previously prepared at home, can often be asked while one answer on unfamiliar material is slowly being elicited.

3. Supplement all questions with slight variations on the basic pattern. If the question is, "What color are your shoes?" ask the next student, "What color is your shirt?" and the next, "What color is your tie?" Also, change the form of the questions wherever indicated to make them more personal and more applicable to your particular class situation. If a question in the book makes use of the impersonal, third-person "John" or "Mary," substitute names of actual members of the class. Try, in short, wherever possible to give the material a natural, lifelike quality. Finally, keep in mind that you are trying to teach *conversation.* Consequently, don't adhere too strictly to the book throughout each lesson. Instead, use the materials of the book as a starting point for conversation. Relate personal experiences connected to something in the text and encourage your students to do likewise. Return to the text only when the conversation lags or seems to have run its course.

Contents

CONTENTS

EXERCISES IN
ENGLISH
CONVERSATION

lesson (1)

At a Motel

"Good evening."

"Good evening. My wife and I would like a room, please. Do you have one available? We don't have a reservation."

"Let me see. (The motel clerk looks through the list of rooms.) Yes, we have one room left. You're lucky. It's the last one. This is our busy season and we're usually full. This one became available because a customer called to cancel a reservation this morning."

"Good. We're tired after driving all day, and we're looking forward to relaxing in a comfortable room."

"This room has two double beds. It's number 25 at the rear of the motel. It's quite a comfortable room. And because it's at the rear, it's far from the noise of the highway."

"How much is it for one night? We only need it for tonight. We're going to continue our trip in the morning."

1

"It's forty dollars a night for two. Is anyone else traveling with you?"

"No, it's just the two of us."

"The air-conditioning switch is on the right as you enter the room. Please turn the air conditioner off when you leave the room. It helps us to keep our electricity bills down."

"I noticed that you have a restaurant attached to the motel. How late is it open?"

"Until eleven o'clock. You have plenty of time. Would you like to pay for the room in cash or with a credit card?"

"Credit card. We don't like to carry much cash with us on our trips." (The customer hands the clerk his credit card. The clerk writes up the bill.)

"Please fill out this registration card. Here is your key. You can park your car in front of your room. Check-out time is noon."

"I'm sure that we'll be on the road before then. Thank you very much."

"Thank you, sir. Enjoy your stay with us."

COMPREHENSION AND CONVERSATION

1. Where does this conversation take place? Between what two people?
2. Why did the clerk tell the customer that he was lucky?
3. What is a *reservation?* How does a person usually make a reservation for a motel or hotel room?
4. Why would someone want to make a reservation in advance?
5. Why did the clerk ask the customer how many people were traveling together?
6. How much did the room cost for two people for one night? How much would a motel room for two people cost in your area?

7. What does *check-out time* mean? What time did the customers at this motel have to check out?

8. Do most motels and hotels have restaurants or coffee shops? How late did this one stay open at night?

9. What was the advantage of having the room at the rear of the motel?

10. How large is a double bed? A single bed? A queen-size bed? Which do you prefer?

11. Do you (or does someone in your family) have a credit card? What kind? What do you use it for?

12. When you travel, do you stay at motels? Describe the experience.

13. Why do you think the customer didn't like to carry cash with him on trips?

14. What is an *air conditioner?* Why did the clerk want the customer to turn it off when he left the room?

15. What are the names of some famous motels or hotels in your area?

PRACTICE DRILL   Tag Endings

John is a good student, *isn't he?* John and Mary are good students, *aren't they?* You like to study, *don't you?* John likes to study English, *doesn't he?* We enjoy our English lessons, *don't we?* John and Mary enjoy their lessons, *don't they?*

You went to the movie last night, *didn't you?* Mary went to the movie last night with you, *didn't she?* John and Mary went to the movie together, *didn't they?*

John was in class yesterday, *wasn't he?* We were very busy yesterday, *weren't we?* John and Mary were also busy, *weren't they?*

You will be here tomorrow, *won't you?* John will also be here tomorrow, *won't he?* Mr. and Mrs. Smith will come to the party, *won't they?*

John can speak English well, *can't he?* You can be here at nine o'clock, *can't you?*

Helen is studying English now, *isn't she?* They are playing tennis now, *aren't they?*

EXERCISE

Add the correct tag endings to the following sentences as shown in the example. Then ask your own questions using tag endings.

Example: *She's the best student in the class, <u>isn't she?</u>*

1. Your friend speaks English well, _____?
2. Mr. Campbell will teach us tomorrow, _____?
3. Your father left for Panama yesterday, _____?
4. He is staying at the Hotel Presidente, _____?
5. Your first name is Robert, _____?
6. The students were late for the lesson, _____?
7. You'll be back by noon, _____?
8. We can speak German, _____?
9. He has a lot of friends, _____?
10. They live in Florida, _____?

VOCABULARY

Use each of these terms in a sentence:
reservation, available, let me see, list, to look through, to have one left, to be lucky, the last one, to become available, to look forward to, to cancel, customer, clerk, to relax, double, rear, quite, to be far from, noise, highway, anyone else, just the two of us, switch, electricity, bill, to notice, to be attached to, plenty of time, credit card, cash, to write up, registration card, to park one's car, on the road, to be sure.

REVIEW

1. Is the United States on the continent of North America or on the continent of South America?
2. What other countries are in North America?
3. Which country lies north of the United States? Which lies south?
4. Does the Atlantic Ocean lie east or west of the United States?
5. When does spring usually begin?
6. In which season of the year does it rain most often? In which does it snow most often?
7. Which is your favorite season of the year? Why?
8. What is the hottest month of the year? The coldest?
9. What is the largest city in the United States?
10. Is New York City larger or smaller than Washington, D.C.?
11. Is it easy or difficult to get a seat on a bus in your city?
12. What is the fare on the bus which you ride?
13. How long does it take you to get to school by bus?
14. What are the colors of the walls in your school?
15. What time did you leave the house this morning? What time will you arrive home this evening?

lesson ②

At a Post Office

"Give me a pack of first-class stamps, please."

"Here you are. That will be five dollars. Anything else?"

"Yes. I want some post cards and some foreign air-mail stamps. I want to send some letters to South America."

"Just a moment, I'll look up the rate for air-mail letters to South America."

"Can you tell me how much it will cost to send a package to Colombia? Also, I want to know how long it will take."

"Do you have the package with you? I would have to weigh it to see how much it would cost. There are several ways to send packages to foreign countries. The fastest way costs the most, of course. I'll give you an example. If you had a two-pound package and you wanted to send it the fastest way, it would cost about six dollars, and it would take about a week to get there."

"Do you insure packages?"

"Yes. All you have to do is declare the value of the package and decide how much you want to insure it for. The rates are reasonable."

"Is there a way that I can be sure that the people in South America receive my package?"

"The post office rarely loses packages. You can, however, request a return receipt. With a return receipt, when the delivery person gives your friend the package, your friend has to sign for it. Then we notify you that he or she has it."

"What about these overnight delivery services I see advertised on television?"

"They're usually as good as the post office, but they may cost more. Also, remember that they only have service within the United States."

"One last question—what are your hours?"

"We open at eight-thirty in the morning and close at five-thirty in the afternoon."

"Thank you, you helped me a lot."

COMPREHENSION AND CONVERSATION

1. Where does this conversation take place? Between what two people?
2. What three items does the customer want to buy?
3. What does *first class* mean? *Air mail?* What is a *post card?*
4. Do you usually send your letters first class? Do you send post cards?
5. How long does it take to send a letter from the United States to Colombia?
6. How long does it take to send a first-class letter from one city to another within your country?

7. How much is a first-class stamp in the United States today? In your country?

8. What did the post office clerk say about sending packages to foreign countries?

9. Why would someone want to insure a package? Is it expensive?

10. Why would someone want to have a return receipt?

11. What is an overnight delivery service? Do you know the names of some of the more famous ones?

12. Is the mail service in the United States good? How is it in your country?

13. When was the last time you sent a letter? Where? Do you send letters to friends in other countries? How much does it cost?

14. When does the post office near you open? When does it close?

15. At the post office you can send letters, buy stamps, and mail packages. What other services are there?

PRACTICE DRILL   Adjectives and Adverbs

John is a *careful* driver. John always drives *carefully*. This is an *easy* exercise. You can do this exercise *easily*. Mary is a *serious* student. She studies English *seriously*. That was a *foolish* thing which Henry did. Henry acted very *foolishly* in that matter. William is a very *bright* boy. The sun shone *brightly* all afternoon. This is a very *slow* train in which we are riding. The train moved *slowly* through the station.

John is a very *fast* worker. He always works *fast*. This is a *hard* exercise for some students. Mary always works *hard*. We must take an *early* train if we want to get there on time. We left home very *early* in the morning.

John works *more seriously* at his English than Mary. I can speak French *more easily* than German. He acted even *more foolishly* than I expected. He has progressed *more rapidly* than anyone else.

John arrived *earlier* than Mary. He arrived *sooner* than we expected. He did *better* in his examination than William. We walked much *farther* along Broadway than they did. He left *later* than we did. She studies much *harder* than she did previously.

EXERCISE

Answer in complete sentences, as in the example.

Example: *Do they work fast or slowly?*
(They work slowly.)

1. Am I speaking slowly or fast?
2. Does Jean do her homework carefully or carelessly?
3. Do you generally walk slowly or rapidly?
4. Do you generally walk more slowly or more rapidly than your friends?
5. Do you usually arrive at school earlier or later than your friends?
6. Does the bus travel more slowly or more rapidly than the subway?
7. Have you progressed in English more rapidly or less rapidly than you expected?
8. Did you do better or worse in your last examination than in your previous examination?
9. Do you usually do well or poorly on examinations in general?
10. Did you leave home this morning earlier or later than usual?
11. Which stops nearer your home, the bus or the subway?
12. Which can you speak more easily, English or your native language?

13. Which can you speak faster, English or your native language?
14. Can you now speak English better or worse than you could two months ago?
15. Which can run more rapidly, a horse or a dog?

VOCABULARY

Use each of these terms in a sentence:
pack, stamp, first class, here you are, post cards, air mail, just a moment, to look up, rate, to weigh, foreign, to give an example, to get somewhere, to insure, to declare, value, reasonable, to receive, rarely, to lose, to request, return receipt, delivery, to sign for, to notify, overnight, to advertise, as good as, within.

REVIEW

1. Is the climate of Florida warmer or colder than that of New York?
2. Is it possible to go swimming in Florida in the winter?
3. Is it possible to go fishing at any time in the United States, or are there special seasons for fishing?
4. What is a game warden?
5. When you travel, do you enjoy sending post cards to your friends?
6. When was the last time you went to the post office? Did you have to stand in line to wait?
7. What is the advantage of sending a post card rather than a letter?
   Which costs less, a letter or a post card?
8. Do you like to go fishing? Hunting? Swimming? Ice-skating? Roller-skating?

9. In what season of the year do people generally go ice-skating?
10. Which is easier, to learn to roller-skate or to learn to ice-skate?
11. Do you skate well? Is skating popular in your country?
12. Where do people go ice-skating in the United States? Do they go in all seasons or in certain seasons only?
13. Do you prefer to go swimming in a pool or in the ocean?
14. Which is easiest for young children, ice-skating, roller-skating, or swimming? Which is safest?
15. Finish this sentence: Roller-skating is better exercise than _____.

lesson ③

English Idioms 1

"Good morning, class. Today we're going to talk about English idioms. Does anyone know what an idiom is?"

"I think I do, Ms. Parks. Isn't an idiom an expression in a language which is difficult to translate into another language?"

"Yes, that's correct, Jane."

"Are there idioms in every language?"

"Every language has its special expressions. If we try to translate them from one language to another, they lose their meaning entirely."

"I speak Spanish as my native language, as you know. Are there idioms in Spanish, too? I don't know of any."

"Most of us are not aware of the idioms in our native language. To us, they are only common everyday expressions. It is only when we study a foreign language that we realize the difficulty and strangeness of some of the expressions."

"Are there many idioms in English?"

"There are hundreds and hundreds.* English is particularly rich in idiomatic expressions."

"Can you give us an example?"

"In the last lesson, the postal clerk said 'I'll look up the rate.' *To look up* doesn't mean to look high into the sky or to look at the roof. It means to search for and find some information. The words don't have an exact translation or equivalent in another language."

"What about the expression *good-bye?* Is that an idiom?"

"That is just a natural, grammatical English expression. It has a direct translation in other languages."

"This is interesting, Ms. Parks. What are some other idioms in English?"

"We'll continue our discussion of idioms in the next lesson. We'll look at some other examples then."

COMPREHENSION AND CONVERSATION

1. Where does this conversation take place? Between what people?
2. What is an *idiom?*
3. Are there idioms in every language or only in certain languages?
4. What happens if we translate an idiom literally from one language to another?
5. Is a person generally conscious of the idioms in his or her native language? Are you?
6. What is your native language? Can you think of an idiom in that language?
7. Are there many idioms in English? Can you think of one?
8. Do you consider the expression *How do you do?* an idiom or just a natural, grammatical English expression?

*See *Essential Idioms in English* by Robert J. Dixson.

9. Do you consider idioms easy or difficult to learn?
10. Is the topic of idioms interesting to you? Was it interesting to the students in the conversation?
11. How can a person become aware of the idioms in his or her native language?
12. When the teacher said, "English is particularly rich in idiomatic expressions," what did she mean by *rich*?
13. What does *to look up* mean?
14. Is *good-bye* an idiom?
15. Find the idiom in this sentence: We'll have to hurry if we're going to be at the theater on time.

PRACTICE DRILL   *good, well,* Comparisons of Equality

John is a *good* student. He always studies *well*. Mary is a *good* singer. She sings very *well*. John and Henry are *good* swimmers. They swim very *well*. Helen is a *good* tennis player. She plays tennis *well*.

John speaks English *as well as* Helen. Can John swim *as fast as* Henry? He always works *as hard as* his sister. You can do it *as easily as* I. I came *as soon as* I could.

Helen does not speak English *as well as* Mary. He doesn't get up *as early as* I. He did not come *as quickly as* we expected. He does not attend class *as regularly as* his sister.

EXERCISE

Answer the questions in complete sentences.
1. Do you want to learn English as quickly as possible?
2. Do you get up on Saturday mornings as early as you do on weekday mornings?
3. Can a dog run as fast as a horse?

4. Do you always do your homework as carefully as possible?
5. Do you speak English as well as the other students in your class?
6. Do you work as hard as your friend or harder?
7. Does she attend class as regularly as her brother?
8. Did we finish this exercise as quickly as you thought we would?

Fill in the blank with *well* or *good.*

9. I'm a _____ student.
10. I speak English _____.
11. Is your pen a _____ one?
12. Jerry is a _____ swimmer.
13. How _____ can your mother speak English?
14. That woman is a _____ singer. How _____ do you sing?
15. Those children play _____ together, don't they?

VOCABULARY

Use each of these terms in a sentence:
idiom, expression, to translate, special, meaning, entirely, as you know, literally, most of us, common, everyday, only, to realize, strangeness, hundreds, particularly, rich, roof, to search for, exact, translation, discussion, to look at, to be conscious of, natural, grammatical, topic, to become aware of, good-bye.

REVIEW

1. When was the last time you had to write an English composition? What was the topic?
2. Is it interesting to write compositions in foreign languages?

3. How much time will you spend on your homework tonight? How much time did you spend last night?
4. What time did you have to get up this morning? What time do you usually get up in the morning?
5. Which do you prefer to read, humorous stories or serious ones?
6. In what century are we living at present? What is the date?
7. What time is it? What time will this class end?
8. Do you like to study geography? Do you know the geography of the United States? Of your country?
9. What is the approximate population of the United States? Of New York City? Of your country?
10. Do you want to learn English as soon as possible?
11. Do you study as much as possible every night?
12. Do you try to get as much practice as possible in conversation?
13. Do you learn as many words as possible every day?
14. Do you know many idioms in English?
15. What does it mean to say that a person speaks a language idiomatically?

lesson ④

English Idioms 2

"Let's talk about idioms again, Ms. Parks."

"All right, Robert, let's do that."

"You said that there were many, many idioms in English. Will you give us some examples?"

"The term *idiom* is a broad one. Many idioms are simply expressions such as *get up, put on, take off,* etc. In other words, they are expressions which we form by adding prepositions to common verbs. When we add prepositions to verbs such as *go, get, come, do, take,* and *make,* they become idiomatic expressions."

"Are all these idiomatic expressions hard to learn?"

"No, they're not too hard to learn if you work hard and study them. They do, however, occur more frequently in spoken English than in written English, and often they do not appear in dictionaries or other reference books."

"Then why are they so important?"

"They're important because we use them constantly in our everyday speech. For example, instead of saying, 'They are *constructing* a new building across the street,' we generally say, 'They are *putting up* a new building across the street.' Instead of saying, 'It took me two weeks to *recover from* my cold,' it is more natural to say, 'It took me two weeks to *get over* my cold.' "

"Why are there so many idiomatic expressions like that?"

"Every language uses its basic, common verbs in a similar way to form idioms. The tendency to do it in English is strong because English comes from Anglo-Saxon. In Anglo-Saxon, new expressions were built on existing words."

"So they added common prepositions to the most common verbs to make new, more complicated verbs."

"That's how it worked, more or less. There are expressions or terms such as *put up, put on, put over, put off, put away,* and even *put up with*—a lot of different verbs which all use the basic verb *put. Take* has *take off, take over, take up, take apart, take down,* and many more. There are similar terms which come from all the common verbs: *do, make, get, come, bring, take,* etc. All these verbs are of Anglo-Saxon origin."

COMPREHENSION AND CONVERSATION

1. Where does this conversation take place? Between what people?
2. Why does the teacher say that the term *idiom* is a broad one?
3. What do the idiomatic expressions *get up, get off,* and *get over* mean?
4. Do you know any other idioms which use the common verb *get?*

5. What happens when we add a preposition to a common verb?

6. How common are idioms in English?

7. What is the difference between spoken English and written English? Why does one have more idiomatic expressions than the other?

8. Why is it important to learn the idioms of English?

9. What does *put up* mean? How is it different from *put up with?*

10. What does *get over* mean?

11. Why does English have so many idioms which use prepositions and common verbs?

12. Are such expressions important or unimportant in English?

13. Can you think of any idiomatic expressions in your language which are similar to those in English?

14. Use these idioms in a sentence: *take over, take off,* and *take apart.*

15. Think of some idioms that use the common verb *make.*

PRACTICE DRILL   Reflexive Pronouns

John is washing the cat. The cat is washing *itself*. I cut the bread with a knife. I cut *myself* yesterday with a knife. Be careful! You will cut *yourself* with that knife. The barber shaves my father every morning, but I prefer to shave *myself*. Do you shave *yourself?* John and I shave *ourselves* every morning. The little girl can dress *herself* very well. She and her little sister dress *themselves* every morning.

I do not study in a class. I study *by myself*. John does not like to eat with us. He prefers to eat *by himself*. Helen works *by herself* in a small office. I do not like to go to the movies *by myself;* I prefer to go with someone. Do you like to go to the movies *by yourself?* My mother often goes to the movies *by herself.*

I *myself* will do the work. Helen *herself* will appear in the play.

John said he *himself* would prepare dinner. We *ourselves* will help you with the work. Miss Smith *herself* will speak to the students.

EXERCISE

Answer these questions in complete sentences, using reflexive pronouns.

1. Do you prefer to study in a group or by yourself?
2. Do most children dress themselves, or do their parents have to help them?
3. At about what age do children learn to dress themselves?
4. Do you come to school every day by yourself, or do you come with someone else?
5. Do you like to talk about yourself?
6. Do I talk about myself too much?
7. Does she study better by herself or with another student?
8. Does he prefer to eat by himself or with others?
9. Are we going to go to the movies by ourselves tonight, or are you going, too?
10. Did they hurt themselves when they fell off the wall?

VOCABULARY

Use each of these terms in a sentence:
let's, broad, in other words, prepositions, frequently, written, spoken, dictionary, reference, to appear, constantly, to construct, across, building, to recover from, natural, basic, similar, tendency, strong, Anglo-Saxon, to express, to add, complicated, more or less, to get up, to get over, to get off, to put up, to put up with, to put on, to put away, to put off, to get over, to take off, to take over, to take apart, to take down, to take up.

REVIEW

1. What are the opposites of the terms *broad, put on, get on,* and *turn on?*
2. What is the difference between a rich and a limited vocabulary? Which does English have?
3. When you no longer want to listen to the radio, do you turn it on or turn it off?
4. Does it take longer to go from Los Angeles to Chicago by train or by plane?
5. How long will it take you to get to school tomorrow? How long did it take you today? How long does it usually take you?
6. How long does it generally take you to get over a cold? Do you get colds often?
7. Do you catch cold more frequently in the winter or in the summer? Why?
8. How long does it take you to do your homework at night? How long did it take you last night?
9. What time do you have to get up every morning? What time will you get up tomorrow morning?

Fill in the blank with *on* or *off.*

10. When I enter a room, I turn the light _____.
11. When I leave a room, I turn the light _____.
12. When the weather is cold, I put my coat _____ before I go out.
13. When I enter a house, I take _____ my hat and coat.
14. She wanted to watch TV, so she turned it _____.
15. I ride the bus for about thirty minutes in the morning, and then I get _____ in front of the school.

lesson (5)

English Idioms 3

"Ms. Parks, in the last lesson you explained that there were many more idioms in spoken English than in written English. Why is that?"

"It's mostly because of habit or tradition, Peter. It seems that whenever people speak English, they use the short, simple, Anglo-Saxon forms which we discussed in the last lesson. In many ways they are more expressive than the longer, more elaborate, Latin words and forms. In writing, however, people seem to use the Latin forms because they seem more literary."

"Is it wrong to use Anglo-Saxon forms when writing or Latin forms when speaking?"

"No, on the contrary. It's perfectly O.K. to use either form when writing or speaking. It's just that the custom is to use the longer form when writing."

"So, there are two languages in English, then, a written one and a spoken one."

"To a certain extent, yes. Actually, this is true in all languages. The written form differs from the spoken form. It is particularly true in English because of the two major origins— Anglo-Saxon and Latin."

"Please give us some more examples of idioms which are used in everyday speech."

"O.K. And I'll try to contrast each with a Latin-form term at the same time. Here's a good one. To *make out* means to *decipher* or to *understand.* It also means to *prepare something,* such as a check. In speaking, we would say, 'The handwriting was so bad that I could not *make out* what it said,' and 'The motel clerk *made out* the receipt for the room.' In writing, those sentences would probably be, 'The handwriting was so bad that I could not decipher what it said,' and 'The desk clerk prepared the receipt for the room.' "

"It seems a little complicated to me."

"It's not. Believe me. You'll become accustomed to it as you study more. Then these words and expressions will seem more interesting and easier to understand. Here's one more. It's the idiomatic expression *to do over.* In speaking it would be common to say, 'The teacher made us *do* our exercises *over* because we made so many mistakes.' In writing, we would probably say, 'The teacher made us *repeat* our exercises because we made so many mistakes.' "

COMPREHENSION AND CONVERSATION

1. Where does this conversation take place? Between what people?
2. Do most idiomatic expressions occur in written English or in spoken English? Why?

3. Which is more difficult for you to understand, written English or spoken English?

4. In speaking, do we use more Anglo-Saxon forms or more Latin forms?

5. Which forms are shorter and simpler? Which are more elaborate and literary?

6. Which forms are the correct ones to use?

7. How can we say that there are two languages, a written English and a spoken English? Is this true for other languages, too?

8. Give two meanings of the term *to make out* as used in spoken English.

9. Give two meanings of the term *to make out* as used in written English.

10. Use the expression *to do over* in spoken English.

11. Use the expression *to do over* in written English.

12. Does this description of idioms in English seem complicated to you? Does it interest you?

13. What other idiomatic expressions do you know that use the common verbs *do* and *make?*

14. Which of the two forms discussed here do you like better? Why?

15. Which do you use more in your native language?

PRACTICE DRILL   Present Perfect Tense 1

I saw that movie last week. I *have seen* that movie. I *have seen* that movie several times. We ate in that restaurant last night. We *have eaten* in that restaurant many times. I mentioned it to him yesterday. I *have mentioned* it to him. I *have mentioned* it to him repeatedly. He went to Chicago on Wednesday. He *has gone* to Chicago. He *has gone* to Chicago many times.

Have you *ever been* to Philadelphia? No, I *have never been* to Philadelphia. I *have been* to Washington several times, but I *have never been* to Philadelphia. *Has* John *come* yet? No, he *hasn't come* yet. Mary and Helen *have arrived,* but we are still waiting for John.

EXERCISE

Answer these questions in complete sentences using the present perfect tense.

1. How many times have you been to the movies this month?
2. Approximately how many times have you gone to the movies this year?
3. Have you ever been to Washington?
4. How many times have you been to Washington?
5. Have you read any good books lately?
6. What good books have you read lately?
7. Have you read any books in English?
8. Have you written many letters or few letters to your friends this year?
9. How many letters have you written to friends this month?
10. Have you written any post cards lately?
11. How many lessons have you studied in this book?
12. How many English lessons have you had so far this week?
13. How many questions have we done in this exercise?
14. How many times has your friend been late to class?
15. Has the teacher asked you for your homework?

VOCABULARY

Use each of these terms in a sentence:
habit, tradition, whenever, expressive, elaborate, literary, form, Latin, on the contrary, to be O.K., custom, to a certain extent, actually, to differ from, origin, to contrast, to make out, to

decipher, to prepare, check, handwriting, so bad, to seem complicated, believe me, to do over, to repeat.

REVIEW

---

1. What are the days of the week? The months of the year?
2. Which is the coldest month of the year? The hottest?
3. When does summer usually begin? Fall?
4. Are you a careful or a careless student? Do you do your work carefully or carelessly?
5. Do you spend much time on your lessons? How much time?
6. Do you use much sugar when you drink coffee or tea?
7. Do you have many friends? Are there many students in your English class?
8. What subjects do you study at school? What subject are you studying now?
9. Who usually teaches you English? Who is teaching you English now?
10. What is your teacher's native language? What language is your teacher speaking now?
11. What is the difference between a habit and a tradition? Is smoking a habit or a tradition?
12. From which ancient languages does English come? What are some of the more important modern languages?
13. In what famous city was Latin spoken?
14. When you want to answer a question in class, do you put your hand up or down?
15. Instead of saying, "That question *arose* last week," what idiom with the verb *come* can we use in place of *arose*?

lesson 6

A Visit from a Foreign Student

"Hello. Are you Mrs. Reese?"

"Yes, I am, and you must be Juan Hernandez. Come in, Juan, we expected you yesterday."

"I'm sorry. I should have called you to say that I couldn't be here until today. There was a problem with my airline ticket, and I couldn't leave until this morning."

"Well, you're here. Let me take your coat. My husband is in the kitchen making coffee. Would you like some?"

"Yes, please. You have a lovely home."

"Thank you. We bought this house seven years ago when we moved here from Mexico City. That's where you're from, isn't it?"

"Yes, it is. I worked for Mr. Reynolds there."

"Of course! Charles Reynolds. How is he? How are his wife and family? I haven't seen the Reynoldses in years."

"They're all fine, Mrs. Reese. Mrs. Reynolds asked me to give you this." (He hands her a gift.)

"Oh, she shouldn't have done that. Oh, how lovely!"

"Mrs. Reynolds also asked me to tell you that she's coming to the States for a short vacation next month, and she hopes that the two of you can renew your friendship. She will write you the details of when they are arriving and how long they'll be able to stay."

"What brings you to California, Juan?"

"I want to take an intensive course in English and then enter a university in the fall."

"But you already speak English quite well. Did you study in Mexico City?"

"Yes, I studied in the public schools for several years. But I have very little practice in speaking. I also have difficulty understanding, especially people who don't speak clearly."

"Well, I hope you'll have the opportunity to practice often with us. And I'm sure that you'll make other friends who will also help you."

"Thank you, you're very kind."

"Oh, here comes Mr. Reese with some coffee."

COMPREHENSION AND CONVERSATION

1. Where does this conversation take place? Between what two people?
2. When did the Reeses expect Juan? Why was he delayed?
3. Where was Mr. Reese?
4. When did the Reeses live in Mexico City? When did Juan leave there?
5. Who is Charles Reynolds? Who knows him?
6. What did Mrs. Reynolds ask Juan to do?
7. What did she ask Juan to tell Mrs. Reese about her travel plans?

8. Why is Juan in California?
9. Have you ever visited California? What is it like?
10. Where did Juan study English? Why does he want to study more English?
11. Do you think Juan knew the Reeses before his arrival? Why?
12. Do you think Juan knew the Reynoldses? Why?
13. Have you ever visited someone that you did not know?
14. Is it a better idea to go to a foreign country to study its language or to stay at home and study it?
15. How do you think Mrs. Reese knew about Juan? (She said she expected him the day before.)

PRACTICE DRILL   *be going* + infinitive

John *is going to study* English next year. We *are going to meet* Fred in Macy's at five o'clock. I *am going to write* a letter to my friend. Helen and Mary *are going to spend* their vacations in Canada. William *is going to visit* some friends in Chicago next week. She *is going to leave* for Europe soon. We *are going to take* a walk in the park after our lesson. John *is going to enter* the university in the fall.

We *were going to play* tennis, but it rained. I *was going to telephone* you last night, but I misplaced your telephone number. We *were going to take* a walk in the park, but it was too cold. I *was going to study* for my examination, but some friends came to visit us. They *were going to go* to Canada on their vacation, but they changed their minds.

EXERCISE

Answer these questions in complete sentences using *be going* plus an infinitive.

1. What is your friend going to do after her lesson today?
2. What time are we going to finish this exercise?
3. Where are you going to have lunch?
4. Are you going to eat with some friends or by yourself?
5. What are you going to do tonight?
6. What is your friend going to do tonight?
7. Are you going to a movie tomorrow night, or are you going to stay at home and study?
8. Where are you going on your vacation?
9. What language are you going to study after you learn English?
10. When is the teacher going to give you an examination in English?

VOCABULARY

Use each of these terms in a sentence:
you must be, problem, airline ticket, husband, kitchen, lovely, ago, to be from somewhere, to work for, in years, to be fine, shouldn't, a short vacation, the two of you, to renew, friendship, detail, intensive, university, already, public schools, especially, opportunity, kind, to be able to.

REVIEW

1. What does Juan say about people who don't speak English clearly? Do you have any difficulties in that area?
2. Do you often have the opportunity to speak English?
3. How long do you think it takes a person to learn to speak a foreign language well? How long do you think it will take you?
4. Why did Juan visit the Reeses?

5. Have you ever stayed with a family in another country?
6. What are the principal geographic sections of the United States?
7. In what geographic section of the United States is New York City? Dallas? Chicago? San Francisco?
8. How many states are there in the United States? Which is the largest? The smallest?
9. What subject are you studying now?
10. In what season of the year does it rain most often?
11. What textbooks have you used to study English? Which one are you using now?
12. What is the name of the person sitting next to you?
13. How much money do you have in your pocket?
14. Where will you go when you leave school today?
15. What time is it?

lesson (7)

The Young Men and the Bull

Once upon a time, two young men were spending some time in the country. One day, while taking a walk together, they crossed a large field.

"Look out!" one of the young men shouted, because a bull suddenly appeared and began to chase them. Naturally they were very frightened. They ran as fast as they could, but the bull kept chasing them.

Finally, one of the men climbed a tree. The other one jumped into a hole, but soon he came out of it. Immediately the bull chased him back into the hole.

"Stay there," his friend shouted, but soon the man came out again, and again the bull chased him right back. This went on five or six more times.

Finally, the man in the tree got angry and shouted to his

friend in the hole, "You fool! Stay in that hole for a while. Otherwise, this bull will keep us here all day!"

"That's easy for you to say," the other man said as he jumped one more time back into the hole, "but there happens to be a bear in this hole."

COMPREHENSION AND CONVERSATION

1. Where does this story take place?
2. Why did the young man shout, "Look out!"
3. When was the last time you shouted, "Look out!" Why did you do this?
4. What happened when the men started running?
5. One man climbed a tree. Where did the other go?
6. What happened five or six times?
7. Why couldn't the man stay in the hole?
8. Why couldn't he stay out of the hole?
9. Have you ever had a problem in which, no matter what you did, there was a danger or difficulty?
10. What did the man in the tree say to his friend in the hole?
11. How did the man who jumped into the hole answer his friend?
12. How do you think the man in the tree felt? How do you think the man in the hole felt?
13. Have you ever seen a bull? A bear? What was it like? Were you frightened?
14. Have you ever been frightened by a wild animal? When?
15. Do you like to spend time in the country? What do you do when you are in the country?

PRACTICE DRILL   Present Perfect Tense 2

John worked there for two years—in 1982 and 1983. John *has worked* there for two years (and is still working there). John studied English for three years when he was in high school. Henry is in our English class; he *has studied* English for two years. Mary was in the hospital for two months last summer. Helen *has been* in the hospital for two months but will come home again next week. Mr. Avona lived in France during the war. My friend *has lived* in France since July. My present English teacher is Mr. Jones; I *have studied* with him for one year. Last year I studied in Miss Lipinski's class.

I *have been studying* English for three years. How long *has* John *been living* in New York? He *has been living* here since the war. I *have been studying* English with Miss Powell, but next week I will study in Mr. Jones's class.

EXERCISE

Answer these questions in complete sentences, using the present perfect tense where appropriate.
1. How long have you been studying English?
2. When did you begin to study English?
3. How long have you been studying with your present teacher?
4. How long did you study English with your previous teacher?
5. How long have you been using this textbook?
6. What English book did you use before you began to use this one?
7. How long have you been living at your present address?
8. How long did you live at your previous address?
9. How many lessons have you studied in this book?
10. Did you find the last lesson easy or difficult?

11. Have you found this lesson easy or difficult?
12. How many English lessons have you had so far this week?
13. How many English lessons did you have last week?
14. How many English lessons have you had so far this month?
15. How many English lessons did you have last month?

VOCABULARY

Use each of these terms in a sentence:
once upon a time, to spend time, Look out!, bull, bear, to chase, naturally, to be frightened, as fast as they could, finally, to jump, hole, immediately, right back, fool, otherwise, there happens to be, hospital, address, country, wild, so far, anecdote, domestic, incident.

REVIEW

1. When you take a walk, do you like to go by yourself or with someone?
2. Why did the young men in the anecdote begin to run when they saw the bull?
3. Have you ever been chased by a bull? Are bulls strong animals or weak ones?
4. Is a bear a strong animal? Which is stronger, a bear or a bull?
5. What is the difference between a wild animal and a domestic one?
6. Name five domestic animals. Name five wild animals.
7. What language is the principal language of Mexico? Of the United States? Of Brazil? Of Japan?
8. What is the capital of England? Of Italy? Of France? Of the Soviet Union? Of Egypt?

9. Do you prefer to study by yourself or with a group?
10. Have you ever hurt yourself seriously with a knife? Describe the incident.
11. Have you ever burned yourself? Has anyone in your family?
12. Do you have many friends who speak English?
13. How much money do you spend on food each day?
14. Do you use much sugar in your coffee or tea?
15. Do you eat much fruit? How many oranges a month do you eat?

lesson (8)

A Love Letter

One day, after receiving a letter from her boyfriend, a young woman called him to say how much she enjoyed the letter.

"It was wonderful, all those beautiful things you said."

"I meant every one of them," the young man replied.

Among other things, he wrote that he loved her and that he thought she was wonderful. The letter was full of poetic thoughts.

"The part I loved most was when you said that in order to be with me, you would suffer the greatest difficulties and face the greatest dangers that anyone could imagine."

"Yes, it's true," he said. "In fact, to spend one minute with you I would climb the highest mountain in the world, I would swim the widest river, I would enter the deepest forest and fight the fiercest animals with my bare hands."

He had written all this in his letter, too.

"There's just one part of the letter that puzzles me," the young woman then said.

"What's that?"

"You signed your name and then added a postscript. Do you remember?"

"Of course. It was important, but I forgot to put it in the body of the letter."

"Your postscript says, 'By the way, I'll be over to see you on Wednesday night—if it doesn't rain.' "

COMPREHENSION AND CONVERSATION

1. What two people were talking on the phone?
2. Why were they talking? Who called whom?
3. What kind of a letter did the young man write?
4. What did he tell his girlfriend in the letter? What kinds of thoughts did he express?
5. What did he mean when he said he would face the greatest dangers?
6. What kinds of dangers was he prepared to face?
7. Did he write all this, or did he say it over the telephone?
8. What part of the letter puzzled the young woman?
9. What is a *postscript?*
10. What did the postscript to this letter say?
11. Why was the postscript amusing and puzzling to the young woman?
12. What does *by the way* mean?
13. Have you ever written a love letter to someone?
14. Has anyone ever written a love letter to you?
15. What do you think of poetic language like that in the young man's letter?

PRACTICE DRILL   Past Continuous Tense

They *were talking* on the telephone when the doorbell rang. *Were* you *doing* your homework last night when I called you? *Were* you *studying,* too?

I *was studying* my lesson when John arrived. We *were having* dinner when you telephoned. John called to me as I *was crossing* the street. While we *were sitting* in the park, we heard a loud cry. It *was raining* hard when we left, but when we got back the sun *was shining.* The game *was* just *beginning* when the mayor and his party arrived. Just as the plane *was leaving* the ground, one of the motors caught fire.

EXERCISE

Answer these questions in complete sentences using the past continuous tense.

1. In the conversation, to whom was the young man talking?
2. What was he talking about?
3. What were you doing at seven o'clock last night?
4. What were you doing at ten o'clock?
5. What were your parents doing last night?
6. When you got up this morning, was the sun shining?
7. What was the teacher doing when you entered the classroom today?
8. Was it raining last week when you went to visit your friend?
9. Was your friend visiting you yesterday when I called on the telephone?
10. Were the students talking when the teacher started this exercise?

VOCABULARY

Use each of these terms in a sentence:
one day, boyfriend, girlfriend, to mean, among other things, to love, wonderful, poetic, in order to, to suffer, to face, danger, to imagine, to be true, in fact, to climb, mountain, forest, bare hands, fierce, just, to puzzle someone, postscript, by the way, telephone, fire, motor, love letter, ever.

REVIEW

1. Have you ever written any poetry? Is it difficult to write poetry?
2. What famous poets do you know who have written their poetry in English?
3. In the young man's letter, he says he would fight the *fiercest animals.* What kinds of animals do we generally consider to be very fierce?
4. He also says he would climb the *highest mountain.* What is the highest mountain in the world? In your country?
5. What is the widest (or longest) river in the world? In your country?
6. In what room are you studying English now? In what room were you studying English last week?
7. In what room will you study English tomorrow?
8. Were you studying English last night at eleven o'clock? If you weren't studying English, what were you doing?
9. Do you take the bus to school every day? Did you take it today? Will you take it tomorrow?
10. How many times this week have you taken the bus to school?
11. Can you run as fast as your friend or faster?

12. Did I arrive as early as you did, or did you arrive earlier?
13. How long have you lived at your present address?
14. How long have you studied English?
15. How long has your friend studied English?

lesson (9)

Schools in the United States 1

"Ms. Parks, the other day you promised to tell us something about the educational system of the United States."

"That's right. I did."

"Are the schools more or less similar everywhere throughout the United States, or do they differ in the various sections?"

"The system of public schools is fairly uniform everywhere throughout the United States, even though the national government has very little to do with it. Each state has its own laws governing education within the state, and each state controls its own schools. Nevertheless, the system everywhere is much the same, and students often transfer from the schools of one state to the schools of another without much difficulty."

"Do most students in the United States attend private schools or public schools?"

"Most public schools in the United States are very good, and the majority of students attend the public schools."

"Which students go to private schools, then?"

"Children needing special instruction, of course; children whose parents can afford to send them to private schools (some are very expensive); and children whose parents want them to receive a religious education. Nonpublic schools enroll about twelve percent of U.S. elementary and high school students."

"But are the public schools good everywhere?"

"No, public schools can be very different. Even in the same city. In the suburbs, public schools are usually quite good, and many parents in the different school districts are very much involved in school activities. Money is available for maintenance, and the buildings are generally modern and well equipped. The teachers are well prepared, too. Some inner-city schools don't have these advantages. But many inner-city schools produce good students in spite of their problems."

"Does it cost anything to attend the public schools? Are there any restrictions as to who may and may not attend?"

"The public schools in the United States are free to everyone, and there is no cost to the student. In most states, even the textbooks are free. There are no restrictions as to color, race, or religion. Any student wishing to attend the public schools may do so."

COMPREHENSION AND CONVERSATION

1. What is this conversation about? What people are talking?
2. Do the schools in the United States differ in the various sections, or are they fairly uniform? Is this also true in your country?
3. Who controls the schools in the United States? In your country?

4. What are the advantages of having the schools under the control of a national government?

5. Do the majority of students in the United States attend public or private schools?

6. Do the majority of students in your country attend public or private schools?

7. Are the public schools in your country good? Are they good in the United States?

8. What kinds of children attend private schools in the United States?

9. What kinds attend private schools in your country?

10. Which do you think is better, to attend a private school or to attend a public school?

11. Which kind do (did) you attend? Do (Did) you like it?

12. What's the difference between a private school and a public school?

13. What are most suburban public school buildings like in the U.S.?

14. Which are more expensive to attend, private or public schools? Which are more popular in your country?

15. What does a person have to do to become a public school teacher?

PRACTICE DRILL   Past Perfect Tense

John said that he *had seen* the movie. When we arrived, Mary *had* already *left.* He *had lived* in France only six months when they left. The movie *had started* when we arrived. I saw immediately that we *had taken* the wrong road. We visited many of the places in Scranton that I *had known* as a young boy. We met many people with whom I *had gone* to school. They *had changed* so much that I was unable to recognize some of them. But some of them mentioned some of the things we *had done* as children, some of the parties we *had attended,* and some of the fine times we *had had* together. Mary was sure that she *had left* her books on the bus.

EXERCISE

Answer these questions in complete sentences using the past perfect tense.
1. At seven o'clock last night, were you having your dinner, or had you already had it?
2. When you arrived at school this morning, how many students had arrived before you?
3. Had the teacher already arrived when you got there?
4. Did your friend say that he had seen the movie or that he had not seen it?
5. Had you studied English before you started this class?
6. How long had you studied English when you began to study in your present class?
7. How long had your friends studied English when they began to study in their present class?
8. When you arrived at the class this morning, had the lesson already begun or had it not begun yet?
9. Had the mail arrived yet when you left home this morning?
10. Had it started to rain when you left home this morning?

VOCABULARY

Use each of these terms in a sentence:
fairly well, just as good as, to have dinner, to have little (or nothing) to do with, much the same, to do so, to arrive at, system, education, fairly, uniform, national, government, law, own, to govern, nevertheless, to transfer, majority, wealthy,

instruction, percent, atmosphere, elegant, exclusive, maintenance, to equip, restriction, race, religion.

REVIEW

1. Give a synonym for *wealthy*. What is its opposite? Its noun form?
2. Are all wealthy people happy? Are all poor people unhappy?
3. Which do you prefer, things that are modern or things that are old-fashioned?
4. What kind of art do you prefer, modern or classical? What kind of music?
5. What were you doing at six o'clock last night?
6. What will you be doing at six o'clock tomorrow night?
7. What were you doing at noon yesterday?
8. What will you be doing at noon tomorrow?
9. By three o'clock this afternoon, will you already have had your English class?
10. If I call you at seven o'clock tonight, what will you be doing? Will you have finished your dinner?
11. How long have you been studying English?
12. How long have you been attending your present school?
13. How long have you lived in the city in which you now live?
14. How long have you been alive?
15. Who is your best friend? How long have you known him or her?

lesson (10)

Schools in the United States 2

"Let's talk some more about schools in the United States, Ms. Parks."

"All right. I find it interesting that each state has its own laws governing education."

"But what about the schools themselves? Are there elementary schools, secondary schools, and colleges—just as in other countries?"

"Yes. Students in the United States begin their education when they're five or six. In some systems, they go to elementary school for eight years and to high school for four. In other systems, they go to elementary school for six years, to junior high school for three years, and to high school for three."

"So that's twelve years of elementary and high school education?"

"That's right. The average student graduates at about age eighteen. There are, of course, different types of high schools. Some are technical, and some are academic. Very often, in the large public high schools, it is possible to select one of several programs. If students plan to go to college, then they take the college preparatory program, which emphasizes literature, mathematics, etc. If they don't plan to go to college, they may take special courses in commercial subjects, home economics, etc. They may also go to a special technical high school and study such things as carpentry or printing."

"How long is the usual college program?"

"The usual college program is four years. To prepare for certain professions, however, more study is necessary. For law, one must now study three more years after college; for medicine, four years after college. Many students, upon finishing the normal four-year course, also take special graduate programs of two or three years' duration in order to specialize in their particular fields."

"Are the colleges, like the elementary and high schools, free to anyone who wishes to attend, or is it necessary to pay in order to attend college?"

"To attend a college or a university, it is usually necessary to pay tuition fees. Many states have their own universities, and these are cheaper for residents of the state. But in most cases, tuition fees are several thousand dollars a year; then there are other expenses, so that it's fairly expensive to go to a college or a university."

"What is the difference between a college and a university?"

"There is really little difference in meaning today. A university is larger than a college and includes several colleges within itself. For example, Columbia University today includes ten or twelve schools or colleges, such as Columbia College, the School of Architecture, the School of the Arts, etc. A smaller school might contain only one or two such divisions, in which case it is usually referred to as a college."

COMPREHENSION AND CONVERSATION

1. What does Ms. Parks find interesting?
2. What is an elementary school? A junior high school? A high school?
3. How many years do children in the United States attend each of these schools?
4. What is the average age of a student who graduates from high school?
5. Are all high schools the same, or are there different types?
6. What are some of the different types of secondary schools?
7. If a student wants to go to college, what types of courses does she or he usually take in high school?
8. If a student does not plan to go to college, what types of courses can he or she take?
9. How long does a student usually attend college?
10. Would you like to (Did you) attend college? For how long?
11. Are most colleges free?
12. What is the difference between a college and a university?
13. What was your favorite subject in elementary school? What was your least favorite?
14. Do all children have to attend elementary school, or is attendance optional?
15. For what different professions can students prepare themselves in college?

PRACTICE DRILL   Passive Voice 1

Our teacher calls the roll every day. Every day the roll *is called* by our teacher. Yesterday our teacher called the roll. Yesterday the roll *was called* by our teacher. Our teacher will call the roll tomorrow. The roll *will be called* by our teacher tomorrow. Our teacher has called the roll every day this week. The roll *has been called* by our teacher every day this week.

This book *was written* by a friend of mine. The money *was taken* by someone in the office. The class *is taught* by Ms. Parks. The letter *has* already *been written*. The food *was eaten* early this morning. The book *will be sent* tomorrow. It *was translated* into English by a friend. He *was married* in January. They *were married* in a church.

EXERCISE

Change these sentences into the passive voice, as in the example.

Example: *We will read the newspaper in class tomorrow.*
            (The newspaper will be read by us in class tomorrow.)

1. Columbus discovered America.
2. Who wrote his book?
3. Ms. Parks teaches the class.
4. Who delivers your mail every day?
5. They will see a play tonight at the theater.
6. Who will call the roll in class tomorrow?
7. They have eaten everything in the refrigerator.
8. Did you write this note?
9. She called me last Tuesday.
10. She calls me every Tuesday.
11. We read the newspaper in class every day.
12. We read the newspaper in class yesterday.
13. My friend wrote this book.
14. Someone in the office took the money.
15. The minister married Dennis and Tonia in a church.

VOCABULARY

Use each of these terms in a sentence:
upon finishing, to be married, such things as, in most cases, to prepare oneself, to graduate from, junior high school, despite, elementary, secondary, to graduate, type, technical, academic, to select, college, preparatory, to emphasize, literature, carpentry, printing, profession, medicine, duration, to specialize, fee, resident, expense, engineer, architecture, division, to discover, optional, doctor, informal.

REVIEW

1. How many years does one have to study in order to become a doctor?
2. Approximately what is the cost of one year's education in a college in the United States? In your country?
3. Do all colleges have the same tuition fees, or do some cost more than others? Why?
4. Give the names of some of the more famous North American colleges and universities.
5. What special tests does one have to take in order to enter a North American college or university?

Be sure you answer the following questions in complete sentences.

6. Do you find these lessons easy or difficult to understand?
7. Were you present or absent from class yesterday?
8. Which do you prefer to study, ancient history or modern history?
9. Has the number of English words in your vocabulary increased or decreased during the past few months?

10. Do you always remember all the new words you study, or do you often forget many of them?
11. Was your textbook cheap or expensive?
12. Do you live near your school or far from it?
13. Do you prefer a formal or an informal atmosphere in which to study English?
14. Did you get a high or a low mark on your last test?
15. Is the street where you live narrow or wide?

lesson (11)

Robert Bruce and the Spider

Robert Bruce was a famous Scottish patriot and general. In the early fourteenth century, he tried to drive the English out of Scotland. But he was unsuccessful because the English were too powerful. Finally, Bruce was forced to run away and to hide in a cave.

One day he lay on a cot in this cave, thinking of the sad state of Scotland. A spider began to weave a web above his head. Simply to amuse himself, Bruce reached up and broke the web. Immediately the spider began to weave a new one. Then six times in succession Bruce broke the web, and six times the spider immediately made a new one. Bruce marveled at such perseverance. He said to himself that he would break the web the seventh time. If the spider made a new one, it would be a good lesson to him, for, like the spider, he had been defeated six times in battle.

Bruce then broke the web, and again the spider made a new one.

From this simple incident, Bruce took heart. He again gathered an army, and this time he was successful in driving out the English.

COMPREHENSION AND CONVERSATION

1. Who was Robert Bruce?
2. What was he trying to do in the fourteenth century? Was he successful at first? Why?
3. What was Bruce finally forced to do? Where did he go?
4. What did he notice while lying on his cot? What was he thinking about while he was lying there?
5. What was the spider's reaction to what Bruce had done?
6. How many times did this activity repeat itself?
7. What lesson did Bruce take from this incident?
8. What happened to him when he gathered a new army?
9. Have you ever learned or taken a lesson from watching an animal? Describe it.
10. What other famous generals do you know of?
11. Whom do you consider the most famous general of all time?
12. Where is Scotland? Is it a small country? What language is spoken there?
13. When did the incident in the story take place? What century are we living in now?
14. Is a spider an insect? Is it large or small?
15. Why are spiders often taken for insects?

PRACTICE DRILL   Passive Voice 2

They are preparing that material now. That material *is being prepared* now. He is writing the letter now. The letter *is being written* now. They were building that road when I was there. That road *was being built* when I was there. He was writing the letter when I was in his office. The letter *was being written* when I was in his office.

We must finish this work at once. This work *must be finished* at once. We must send these letters today. These letters *must be sent* today. We can use this room for our lesson. This room *can be used* for our lesson. You should study this exercise for tomorrow. This exercise *should be studied* for tomorrow. They should mail this letter immediately. These letters *should be mailed* immediately. We have to do this today. This *has to be done* today. He has to sign those papers before he leaves. These papers *have to be signed* before he leaves.

EXERCISE

Answer these questions in complete sentences using the passive voice.

1. In what room is your English class being given today?
2. By whom is the class being taught?
3. How many new words must be studied in each of these lessons?
4. Can English be learned well in six months?
5. Should the windows be left open, or should they be closed during a storm?
6. Is this question being answered now?
7. At what time can you always be reached by phone?
8. In what kind of store can men's shirts be bought?

9. In what kind of store can fruit be bought? Eggs? Bread? Shoes? Newspapers?
10. Should certain exercises in this book be studied more carefully than others?
11. When must the homework be finished?
12. Why must these letters be sent?
13. When should this exercise be studied?
14. When does her will have to be signed?
15. When can this room be used for something else?

VOCABULARY

Use each of these terms in a sentence:
to run away, to say to oneself, at once, to think of, to take heart, to reach up, to be successful in, in succession, to drive out, reaction, to be forced to, Scottish, patriot, century, to try, Scotland, unsuccessful, powerful, to force, cave, cot, spider, to weave, web, head, to amuse, to break, succession, to marvel, to defeat, battle, incident, heart, to gather, successful, material, to build, storm, quality, character, insect, to obtain.

REVIEW

1. What are the days of the week? The months of the year?
2. How many hours are there in a day?
3. How many days in a week? A month? A year?
4. What are we doing now? What were we doing an hour ago?
5. What will you be doing at this time tomorrow?
6. What were you doing at eight o'clock last night?
7. Do you find English verb forms easy or difficult?
8. Give the principal parts of the verbs go, take, and be.

9. Is English grammar similar to Spanish grammar? Which do you think is easier?
10. Is New York City smaller or larger than Washington, D.C.?
11. Which is the largest city, New York, Washington, or Chicago?
12. Was this textbook more or less expensive than the others you have had to buy?
13. Who is the tallest person in your class? The shortest?
14. Who came to class the earliest this morning? Who came the latest?
15. Have you ever been in this room by yourself?

lesson (12)

A Lucky Escape

There is another story of a spider which is rather interesting. It concerns a certain general of ancient times who had lost a battle and, in the company of a faithful servant, was trying to escape from the enemy. Both were extremely tired, and both were hungry and thirsty, but they did not dare to go into any town for fear of being discovered and captured by the enemy.

Toward evening, they arrived at a mountain where there was a small cave.

"Let us hide here," said the servant. "Perhaps if those who are following us lose our trail, we shall be able to escape."

"No. I think that the hate which they feel toward us will make them more alert, and that they will find us wherever we are."

But they entered deep into the cave and remained there.

In the morning, they heard steps nearby. A group of soldiers was approaching the entrance to the cave.

"Let's look in here," said one of the soldiers, getting ready to enter the cave.

"Don't be foolish," said another. "No one has entered here."

"How do you know?"

"Don't you have eyes?" said the other. "Don't you see the large spider's web that covers the entrance from one side to the other? How could anyone enter?"

Everyone then looked and saw that there was really a spider's web which completely covered the entrance.

"It's true," they said.

And they continued on their way.

The general and his servant looked at each other with great surprise. The entire thing seemed to be a miracle. They were both alive, and they owed their lives to the fact that during the night a simple spider had woven a web completely across the entrance to their cave.

COMPREHENSION AND CONVERSATION

1. Who is this story about? Did the event take place recently?
2. With whom was the general traveling? Where were they going?
3. Why were they tired?
4. Why couldn't they go into town? Who was following them?
5. Where did they hide? Why did they choose that place?
6. What was the general's opinion about entering the cave?
7. What happened the next morning?
8. Why did the soldiers decide not to enter the cave to look for the two men?
9. What was the reaction of the two men in the cave?
10. Can a spider weave a web quickly, or does it take a long time?
11. Do you think it is possible for a spider to weave a web large enough to cover the entrance of a cave in one night?
12. What kinds of animals sometimes make their homes in

caves? Did people ever make their homes in caves? What people?

13. What is a miracle? Why did the general and his servant consider the event to be a miracle?

14. Do you think the anecdote was true or just a story?

15. Have you ever had to hide from someone? Describe the incident.

PRACTICE DRILL   Sequence of Tenses

In the story the soldier *says* that a spider's web *covers* the entrance. In the story the soldier *said* that a spider's web *covered* the entrance. He *says* that it *will be* foolish to enter the cave. He *said* that it *would be* foolish to enter the cave. The general *says* he *is* tired. The general *said* he *was* tired.

She *says* she *will arrive* at six o'clock. She *said* she *would arrive* at six o'clock. They *think* we *are leaving* soon. They *thought* we *were leaving* soon. She *says* she's *studied* English for many years. She *said* she'd *studied* English for many years. I *think* I *can meet* you at noon. I *thought* I *could meet* you at noon.

EXERCISE

Use the correct sequence of tenses in answering these questions.

1. Did the general in the story think it was wise or foolish to enter the cave?

2. Did he think he and his servant would be captured by the enemy?

3. Did the soldiers think it would be possible for someone to enter the cave without breaking the web?

4. To what did the general and his servant think they owed their lives?

5. What does the newspaper say the weather will be tomorrow?
6. Did you say you were coming to class tomorrow?
7. When did your teacher say she or he was going to give you a test?
8. Does your friend say he or she can speak English well?
9. Did your teacher say he or she had studied English for many years?
10. When did your aunt say she would arrive?

VOCABULARY

Use each of these terms in a sentence:
for fear of, to get ready, a long time, toward evening, a short time, to take a long time, at noon.

REVIEW

1. Do you often ride the bus to school?
2. When was the last time you took the bus to school?
3. What is the fare on the bus? Is it cheaper than any other means of transportation?
4. Do the buses stop at every corner or only at certain corners? How are these corners marked?
5. What colors are the buses in your city painted?
6. Do you always get a seat on the bus, or do you sometimes have to stand?
7. Are transfers given free on the buses in your city, or do you have to pay for them?
8. At what hours of the day are the buses most crowded? Least crowded?
9. Are there many taxis in your city? What colors are they painted?

10. Is it expensive to ride in taxis in your city?
11. Do the taxis in your city charge by the mile or by the trip?
12. What is the most rapid means of transportation in your city?
13. What is the cheapest means of transportation?
14. What is your favorite means of transportation?
15. How would you like to drive a bus? A taxi?

lesson (13)

Holidays in the United States

"Ms. Parks, my grandparents visited the United States a few months ago. When they came back, they told us about a holiday called Thanksgiving. Will you tell us about Thanksgiving, please?"

"Yes, and about the other holidays in the United States, too."

"I'd be happy to. The most important holidays are Christmas, Easter, Thanksgiving, Independence Day, Memorial Day, and Labor Day."

"I've heard of Christmas and Easter, of course, since we celebrate them here, too. In fact, aren't they celebrated in all countries?"

"In the West, yes. The manner of celebrating Christmas and Easter differs in various countries, but they are celebrated everywhere in the West on the same day."

"What about the one Jan's grandparents told her about—Thanksgiving?"

"Thanksgiving Day is a special American holiday, always celebrated on the fourth Thursday of November. It is a holiday first celebrated by the Pilgrims, who were some of the first settlers of the United States. They set aside this day as a day of thanks to the Lord for the help they had received in overcoming the many difficulties of establishing their homes here. The day continues to be a day of thanks for the continued growth and prosperity of the country."

"And Independence Day? On what day is Independence Day celebrated?"

"Independence Day is celebrated on the fourth of July because on that day in the year 1776, the Declaration of Independence was signed. At that time, the thirteen original colonies separated from England and became an independent country."

"What other important holidays are there in the United States?"

"There is Memorial Day, which is observed on May 30. This day is set aside in memory of the many soldiers who have died in the several wars in which the United States took part. There is also Labor Day, the first Monday in September. This is a day of rest dedicated to the working people of the country. These two holidays also serve as the traditional beginning and end of the summer vacation period for students. Millions of people go to seashore and mountain resorts to celebrate the start and finish of summer."

"Are there any holidays which honor specific people in your nation's history?"

"Certainly. These are not as major as the holidays I just mentioned, but they are important, too. There's Martin Luther King's birthday on January 15, Abraham Lincoln's birthday on February 12, George Washington's birthday on February 22, and Columbus Day on October 12. There are many minor holidays, too, such as Valentine's Day, February 14; Halloween, October 31; Saint Patrick's Day, March 17; and several others."

COMPREHENSION AND CONVERSATION

1. What are the most important holidays in the United States?
2. What are the most important national holidays in your country?
3. Do you think the people of the United States celebrate Christmas and Easter the same as the people of your country?
4. Who first established the custom of celebrating Thanksgiving Day?
5. Who were the Pilgrims?
6. How many colonies were in the original United States?
7. What minor holidays, in addition to the major holidays, are also celebrated in the United States?
8. What is Memorial Day?
9. To whom is Labor Day dedicated? On what date is it?
10. What happened of historical importance on July 4, 1776? How is this day celebrated?
11. The birthdays of what famous people are celebrated in the first two months of the year?
12. Who was the commander in chief of the American forces during the American Revolution?
13. Who was the first president of the United States? Who is the president today?
14. Who was the president during the American Civil War?
15. What is your favorite holiday? Why?

PRACTICE DRILL   *supposed to*

The lesson *is supposed to* begin at nine o'clock, but sometimes we do not begin until later. They *are supposed to* deliver the merchandise this afternoon. I *am supposed to* meet Mary tonight at the movies. At what time *is* the lecture *supposed to* begin? It *is supposed to* begin at nine o'clock. Where *are* the students *supposed to* leave their books when they go to lunch? They *are* *supposed to* leave them on their desks.

EXERCISE

Answer these questions using the correct form of *supposed to.*
1. At what time is your English lesson supposed to begin?
2. At what time is your lesson supposed to end?
3. How long is your lesson supposed to last?
4. How long are you supposed to spend on your homework each night?
5. At what time are you supposed to leave home each morning?
6. At what time are you supposed to arrive at school?
7. What are you supposed to do if you arrive late for class?
8. When you finish studying this book, are you supposed to begin studying a new one?
9. What time is the movie supposed to start tonight?
10. What am I supposed to do when I finish this exercise?

VOCABULARY

Use each of these terms in a sentence:
to set aside, in memory of, to be happy to, to hear of, in fact, traditional, vacation, seashore, resort, holiday, to celebrate, to set aside, to receive, to overcome, to establish, growth, prosperity, original, colony, memory, to die, to dedicate, laborer, ship, to sail, to deliver, merchandise, lecture, heroes, customary, exchange, ceremony, to compose, to hold, star, extensive, to observe.

REVIEW

1. Where does your family go on vacation?
2. Which do you prefer, the mountains or the seashore?
3. Have you been to the movies this week? This month? How many times?
4. Who is your favorite movie star?
5. How long have you studied English?
6. How long have you been in your present class?
7. How long had you studied English when you entered your present class?
8. Did you know your present English teacher when you began to study in your present class?
9. How long have you lived at your present address? How long at your previous address?
10. Since what approximate date have you been using this book?
11. How many lessons have you completed in this book? How many are left to do?
12. On what approximate date are you supposed to finish this book?
13. Have you been studying English as long as your friend?
14. What foreign cities have you visited?
15. What famous museums have you visited?

lesson (14)

The Young Prince

Once upon a time, there was a young prince who became quite ill. As a result of his illness, he developed some rather strange ideas. For example, he became convinced that he was a cow. Since it was the practice in his religion to sacrifice cows, he then insisted on being sacrificed like all other cows. Many famous doctors were called in to treat him, but none of them was able to help him. Finally, after all the others had failed, an old village doctor was called. The old doctor, after considering the case carefully, began to pretend that he was the village priest and that he had come to sacrifice the prince. He took out a long knife and began to feel the prince's arms and legs in order to find the best place to cut him. Then he suddenly stopped.

"I cannot cut this animal to offer it as sacrifice to the gods," he said. "This animal is much too thin and weak to sacrifice. It would be an insult to offer such a poor specimen."

The prince was naturally very much disturbed. "But you must," he insisted.

"Surely you agree with me, Your Highness," persisted the old doctor.

"If I must get fatter, then I shall do so," the prince finally agreed. He therefore began to eat and drink large quantities of food. He ate and ate, and, as the weeks passed, he became much fatter. But at the same time, his strength also increased, and his health improved. In fact, he soon felt so much better that he forgot all about being a cow.

COMPREHENSION AND CONVERSATION

1. Why did the young prince begin to think he was a cow?
2. Are there many cows in your country?
3. Is a cow a domestic animal or a wild animal? What are cows used for?
4. What other animals are useful to people? Are all of them domestic?
5. Why did the prince insist on being sacrificed? Who was called in to deal with this problem?
6. What did the old doctor decide to do to help the prince?
7. Why did he begin to feel the prince's arms and legs?
8. What did he say just before he was to cut into the prince?
9. How did the prince respond?
10. What did the prince do next? How did he begin to forget about being a cow?
11. What do you think of the old doctor's method of treating the young prince? Was it effective?
12. What religions sacrifice (or sacrificed) animals to their gods?
13. In what way was the old doctor wiser than the famous doctors who were called in first?

14. Why do you think the young prince decided to cooperate with the old doctor?
15. If you could be any animal, which would you want to be?

PRACTICE DRILL   Present Tense after Conditionals

If Harry *studies* (not *will study*) hard, he will pass this course. If Doris *comes* before six o'clock, I can talk to her. If it *doesn't rain* tomorrow, we will go to the park. If he *is* late, he will have to wait to see the doctor. If he *likes* the house, they are going to buy it. If he *does not come soon*, we will have to leave without him.

When Mary *comes*, we will tell her all about it. *As soon as* John *arrives*, we will leave. He says he will wait here *until* Mary *telephones*. Call me *as soon as* he *gets* here. I will not go *unless* William *goes* with me.

EXERCISE

Answer these questions in complete sentences.
1. If it rains tomorrow, will you go to your English class as usual?
2. If it rains tonight, will you study at home, or will you go to a movie?
3. When you finish studying English, will you begin to study another foreign language?
4. When you finish using this book, will you begin immediately to study another?
5. As soon as you finish your homework, will you go to bed?
6. If you get up late tomorrow, will you arrive at school in time for your lesson?
7. Will you wait for me until I finish my work this afternoon?

8. What will you do if your friend doesn't call you about the concert tickets?
9. Will you have dinner as soon as you arrive home, or will you read or watch TV first?
10. If you can't go to the dance this weekend, what will you tell your friend?

VOCABULARY

Use each of these terms in a sentence:
to get fat, to call in, to insist on, to become convinced, gods, Your Highness, to persist, surely, prince, princess, result, to convince, to practice, to sacrifice, to insist, to treat, to fail, to pretend, priest, leg, animal, then, insult, to disturb, fat, quantity, strength, to increase, health, to improve, to succeed, unless, excuse, to oppose, to cooperate, to resist, to approve, to disapprove, instrument.

REVIEW

1. What time is your English lesson supposed to begin? To end?
2. What time are you supposed to arrive at school each day? What time are you supposed to leave?
3. How much time are you supposed to spend on your homework each night?
4. Which kinds of animals are supposed to be more useful to people, domestic or wild?
5. Name ten wild animals. Which is the largest? The fastest?
6. Which is supposed to be faster, a taxi or a bus?
7. Which is supposed to be able to run faster, a dog or a horse?
8. When does the schedule say the movie is supposed to start?

9. When did your teacher tell you this class was supposed to end?
10. Who is your teacher? Who used to be your teacher?
11. What book did you use to use?
12. Have you always lived in the same house, or did you use to live somewhere else?
13. When you were younger, what games did you use to play?
14. What time is it? What time was it an hour ago?
15. How much is two plus eleven minus four?

lesson (15)

A Fable by Aesop

One of the fables by the ancient Greek writer Aesop concerns a group of animals who, one day, were discussing the popularity of the elephant. They all agreed that the elephant was the most popular animal in the forest, but none of them could give a satisfactory explanation for this fact.

The giraffe said, "If the elephant had a long neck like mine, then it would be easy to understand his popularity. He would be the tallest animal in the forest."

The peacock said, "If the elephant had a beautiful tail like mine, it would be easy to understand. He would be the most beautiful animal in the forest."

The rabbit said, "If the elephant could run as fast as I, it would be easy to understand. He would be the fastest animal in the forest."

The bear said, "If the elephant were as strong as I, it would be easy to understand. He would be the strongest animal in the forest."

Suddenly the elephant himself appeared.

"Your neck is not as long as mine," said the giraffe. But the elephant said nothing.

"Your tail is not nearly as beautiful as mine," said the peacock. But the elephant said nothing.

"I could run a circle around you and still win a race," said the rabbit. Still the elephant said nothing.

"My arms are more limber and stronger than yours," said the bear. But the elephant stood silently. He was larger and stronger than any of the other animals; indeed, he was superior in many other ways. But he was always quiet and modest about his many accomplishments.

This, after all, was the real explanation of his popularity.

COMPREHENSION AND CONVERSATION

1. Who was Aesop? What is a *fable?*
2. What were the animals discussing?
3. Are elephants large or small animals? Are they wild or domestic?
4. Is it possible to tame an elephant? What other wild animals can be tamed?
5. Why couldn't the giraffe understand the elephant's popularity? Why couldn't the peacock understand it? The rabbit? The bear?
6. Which is taller, an elephant or a giraffe?
7. Which is faster, a rabbit or an elephant?
8. Which is stronger, a bear or an elephant?
9. Which animal has a more beautiful tail, a peacock or an elephant?
10. What did the animals say when the elephant appeared?

11. How did the elephant respond to their observations?
12. What was the real explanation of the elephant's popularity?
13. Most of Aesop's fables have a moral. What is the moral of this one?
14. What other fables of Aesop do you know? Do you enjoy reading them or hearing them? Do you enjoy their morals?
15. Would you like to be a person who is quiet and modest about your accomplishments, or do you think you should be more openly proud?

PRACTICE DRILL   Conditionals 1

Ken doesn't have a car, but if he *had* a car, he *would drive* to the beach each Sunday. I don't have the time, but if I *had* more time, I *would study* French. If he *knew* how to drive, he *would borrow* his uncle's car. If the weather *were* nice today, we *would go* to the park. If he *prepared* his lessons every night, he *would receive* better marks. She *would make* more progress if she *studied* more. I *would go* with you if I *were* not so busy. If he *went* to bed earlier each night and *got* more sleep, he *would feel* better. He *could come* with us if he *wanted* to. If we *had* more practice in conversation, we *would be* able to speak more fluently. The bear said that if the elephant *were* as strong as he, it *would be* easy to understand his popularity. If the elephant *had* a long neck like the giraffe, he naturally *would be* much taller.

EXERCISE

Answer these questions in complete sentences.
1. Would you speak English more fluently if you had more daily conversation practice?
2. If you had a lot of free time, would you go to the movies less often or more often?

3. If you could speak English well, would you continue to study, or would you give up studying?

4. If you did your homework more carefully, would you get better marks?

5. If there were more students in your class, would you have more opportunity or less opportunity to speak English?

6. If today were Sunday, where would you go and what would you do?

7. If today were a holiday, where would you go and what would you do?

8. If you were a millionaire, do you think you would be happier than you are at present?

9. If you didn't have to work or study, how would you spend your time?

10. If you were in Florida now, what would you do?

11. If you knew English perfectly, what other language would you begin to study?

12. If you had a new car, where would you drive this weekend?

13. If you were on vacation now, how would you spend your time?

14. If you could visit any country in the world, what country would you go to?

15. If there were an elephant in this classroom, where would it sit?

VOCABULARY

Use each of these terms in a sentence:
fable, circle, limber, indeed, silently, after all, at present, to know how, weekend, to be concerned with, to give up, Greek, popularity, elephant, satisfactory, explanation, giraffe, neck, peacock, tail, rabbit, modest, accomplishment, latter, to compare, beach, to borrow, uncle, vain, mark, fluently, millionaire, to assume, condition, to domesticate, to tame, moral.

REVIEW

1. Which month precedes February? Which month follows February? How many days are there in February?
2. What are the four seasons of the year? Which is the hottest in the United States?
3. In which season of the year do people in the United States go swimming? In which do they go ice-skating?
4. What is the largest city in Mexico? What language is spoken there? What ocean is west of Mexico?
5. What are the principal languages spoken in the following countries: France, Egypt, the Soviet Union, Italy?
6. What subjects are you studying in school at present? Which is your favorite?
7. Does English grammar seem easy to you? What about English pronunciation? Spelling?
8. If you could speak English perfectly, what English-speaking countries would you like to visit?
9. Which is larger, Brazil or Mexico? Canada or Colombia?
10. What other languages besides English would you like to be able to speak?
11. Do you wear a wrist watch? Of what material is it made? What time is it now?
12. What was the name of the last movie you saw? Who starred in it? Did you like it?
13. Do you often watch TV? What is the name of your favorite show? Who are the stars?
14. Have you ever played any video games? Which ones? Do you enjoy playing video games?
15. How many lessons have we completed in this book? How many students are in this class? How many people are there in your family?

lesson (16)

The Farmer and the Apple Tree

A poor farmer once had a friend who was famous for the wonderful apple trees that she grew. The farmer went to visit his friend one fine day in the spring.

As the farmer was about to leave, his friend said, "Here is a young apple tree. I want you to take it home and plant it. I want you and your family to enjoy it."

The farmer was pleased. "Thank you very much," he said. "I know this tree will bear fine apples."

But when the farmer got home, he did not know where to plant the tree. He was afraid that if he planted it near the road, strangers would steal the fruit. If he planted it in one of his fields, his neighbors would come at night and steal some of the apples. If he planted it near his house, his children would take the fruit. Finally, he planted the tree deep in his woods, where

78

no one could see it. But, naturally, without sunlight and proper soil, it soon died.

Later that year, the friend who had given the farmer the tree went over to his farm to visit. Naturally, she inquired about the tree.

"Why did you plant the tree in such a poor place?" she asked, puzzled.

"What's the difference?" the farmer said angrily. "If I had planted the tree near the road, strangers would have stolen the fruit. If I had planted the tree in one of my fields, my neighbors would have come at night and stolen some of the apples. If I had planted it near my house, my own children would have taken the fruit."

"Yes," said the friend. "But at least someone could have enjoyed the fruit. Now, by your foolish action, you have robbed everyone of the fruit, and you have also destroyed a good tree."

COMPREHENSION AND CONVERSATION

1. What was the friend of the poor farmer famous for? When did he visit her?
2. What did the friend give the farmer? What did she tell him to do with the gift?
3. Why was the farmer afraid to plant the tree near the road?
4. What did he think would happen if he planted it in one of his fields? What did he think would happen if he planted it near his house?
5. Where did he finally plant the tree? Why?
6. What happened to the tree without sunlight and proper soil? What do trees need in order to grow properly?
7. What happened when the farmer's friend went over to visit him later in the year? What did she ask him?
8. How did he explain his actions?
9. What was her response?

10. Do you think the farmer acted wisely or foolishly? What should he have done?
11. Do all trees grow easily? What is the proper season for planting trees? In what season do they bear fruit?
12. Name some common fruit trees in English.
13. What is your favorite kind of fruit?
14. If you cut open an apple, what do you find inside? What do we call the outer covering of an apple?
15. What do you think the message (or moral) of this story is? How does it compare with the moral of the last story?

PRACTICE DRILL   Conditionals 2

If the farmer *had planted* the tree in a better place, the tree *would have grown* well. If I *had known* your telephone number, I *would have called* you up last night. If the weather *had been* warm yesterday, they *would have gone* to the beach. If he *had taken* a taxi, he *would have caught* the train. If John *had worn* his overcoat, he *would not have caught* cold. We *could have gone* if they *had invited* us. If he *had mentioned* it in time, we *could have saved* ourselves all that trouble. If I *had been* in your place, I *would have gone* with him.

EXERCISE

Answer these questions using the appropriate conditional forms.
1. If yesterday had been a holiday, where would you have spent the day?
2. If you had begun to study English years ago, would you have had to take this course?
3. If you had been in Florida last winter, how would you have spent your time?

4. If you had had more time to prepare your lessons, would you have made more progress or less progress in English?

5. If the farmer in the anecdote had planted the tree in a good place, would the tree probably have grown well?

6. If he had planted the tree near the road, do you think strangers would have stolen the fruit?

7. If you had gotten up late this morning, would you have arrived at school on time, or would you have been late?

8. If yesterday had been Sunday, would you have gone to school as usual, or would you have spent the day in some other way?

9. If you had been born in Spain, what language would you have learned as a child?

10. If you had been born in France, what language would you probably be able to speak well now?

11. If you could have taken a trip to Europe last summer, what countries would you have visited?

12. If you had had a car last weekend, where would you have gone?

13. If you had been free to go to the movies last evening, what film would you have gone to see?

14. If it had rained yesterday, would you have used your umbrella?

15. If we had begun this lesson two hours ago, would we have finished by now?

VOCABULARY

Use each of these terms in a sentence:
to be famous for, apple, to be about to leave, to inquire about, to be pleased, What's the difference?, to save oneself the trouble, at night, to rob someone of, at least.

REVIEW Past Tense Irregular Verbs

1. At what time did your English lesson begin today?
2. Where did you buy your English book? How much did it cost? How much did you pay for it?
3. How many books did you bring to school with you today?
4. When was the last time you caught cold?
5. What time did you come to school today?
6. What time did you get up? What time did you leave home?
7. How much time did you spend doing your homework last night?
8. When you left home this morning, did you put your coat on or take it off?
9. How many hours did you sleep last night?
10. Did you speak English well before you started this course?
11. When did you last see your cousin? When did you last write to him or her?
12. What articles did you read in the newspaper yesterday?
13. Did you make many mistakes on your last exam?
14. What time did you eat dinner last night?
15. How many glasses of water did you drink yesterday?

lesson (17)

The Three Wishes

Long ago, there lived a couple who had a dairy farm. They were poor and spent much of their time wishing for things they did not have.

Often the man would say, "I wish I were handsome," or "I wish I had more cows."

Frequently the woman would say, "I wish I were wealthy," or "I wish I were a beautiful princess."

One day, some fairies heard their wishes and decided to conduct an experiment. They went to the couple and granted them three wishes. Whatever they wished would truly be granted.

The couple talked a long time over what they should wish for. But after a while they became hungry, and from force of habit the woman suddenly said, "I wish I had some sausages to eat."

Immediately her market basket was full of sausages.

Then a heated argument began because the husband said that his wife had wasted one of their valuable wishes on such a cheap thing as sausages. The argument grew hotter, and finally in anger the wife said, "I wish these sausages were hanging from your nose!"

Of course the sausages immediately flew to the poor man's nose and stayed there. Nor could they be removed. Now, there was only one thing the poor woman could do. She really loved her husband, and so she had to spend their third wish in removing the sausages from his nose. Thus, except for a few sausages, they had nothing to show for their three wishes.

COMPREHENSION AND CONVERSATION

1. What is a *dairy farm*? What kind of animals live on such a farm?
2. Did this couple spend much of their time wishing? How did they express their wishes?
3. Do you often wish for things you do not possess?
4. What did the fairies decide? What is a *fairy*? Do you think there are such things as fairies?
5. Why did the farm couple talk about their wishes a long time?
6. What happened when the woman got hungry? If you had been hungry, what would you have wished for?
7. What happened when the woman wished for the food?
8. Why did the husband and wife begin arguing?
9. What happened then to the string of sausages?
10. How did the couple have to use their third wish?
11. What is the moral of this story?
12. When you were young, did you spend much time reading fairy tales?
13. Do you think that fairy tales are good for children to read?

14. What does the phrase *force of habit* mean?
15. Give some examples of things you do from force of habit.

PRACTICE DRILL   Subjunctive after *wish*

The farmer wishes they *were* wealthy. He wishes he *were* handsome, and she wishes she *were* beautiful. I wish I *could speak* English well. I wish Maryanne *were* here now; she could help us with this problem. Hal wishes he *knew* how to cook well. I wish I *had started* to study Spanish many years ago. I wish I *had gone* to the movies with you last night; my brother told me the film was very good. I wish I *were* in Florida now; I would go swimming at the beach. I wish I *had been* in Florida with you last month; I would have gone swimming every day. I don't like the rain; I wish it *were not* raining now.

EXERCISE

Answer these questions in complete sentences using the appropriate subjunctive form.
1. Do you wish you were in California now? What would you do if you were there?
2. Do you wish you had been in California last winter? What would you have done if you had been there?
3. Do you wish you could speak English perfectly?
4. Do you wish you had started to study English a long time ago?
5. If you had studied English a long time ago, would you be able to speak much more fluently now?
6. Do you wish you could speak English as well as your teacher?
7. Would you like to be able to speak several languages?

8. Do you wish you were very wealthy, or would you prefer to be poor?
9. Do you wish you were much younger than you are, or do you wish you were older?
10. Do you wish you could swim well? What else do you wish you could do well?

VOCABULARY

Use each of these terms in a sentence:
to wish for, from force of habit, long ago, dairy, cow, princess, to conduct, to grant, frequently, fairy, experiment, truly, to become hungry, sausage, market basket, husband, handsome, nose, in anger, to grow hotter, heated, to be hanging from, nothing to show for, to waste.

REVIEW

1. How do you spend most of your time on Sundays?
2. How do you spend most of your time during the summer?
3. What is a habit? What is the difference between a habit and a custom?
4. What are some habits that you consider to be good habits? What are some bad habits?
5. Did the three wishes that the fairies granted turn out to be valuable or valueless? What is the noun form of the adjective *valuable?*
6. Which is more valuable, gold or silver?
7. Which is more valuable, a nickel or a dime?
8. How many letters are there in the English alphabet? How many symbols are there in the writing system of your native language?

9. How many vowels are there in the English alphabet? How many consonants?
10. What letter precedes *m* in the English alphabet? What letter follows *m?*
11. Do you study English by youself or in a group?
12. Do most men shave themselves, or do they go to a barber?
13. Have you ever burned yourself badly? When?
14. Do you live by yourself or with your family?
15. Have you ever traveled by yourself, or do you always travel with someone?

lesson 18

The Arab
and the Camel

An Arab was walking alone through the desert when he met two merchants.

"Have you lost one of your camels?" he asked them.

"Yes," they answered.

"Was he blind in the right eye and lame in the left foot?" the Arab asked.

"Yes, he was."

"Had he lost a tooth?" asked the Arab.

"Yes."

"Was he carrying a load of honey and of corn?"

"Yes," said the merchants. "Please tell us where he is."

"I don't know where he is," said the Arab. "I have never seen such a camel, nor have I talked with anyone about him."

The merchants looked at each other with surprise. They

thought that the man was deceiving them. Finally, they came up close to him, took hold of him, and said, "Where is the camel, and what have you done with the jewels which were hidden in the cargo?"

"I have seen neither the camel, nor the cargo, nor the jewels," insisted the Arab.

The merchants finally forced the man to accompany them to a nearby town, and there they led him before a police officer. The merchants claimed that the man was either a thief or a magician.

"I am neither a thief nor a magician," said the Arab. "Nor am I an educated man. But, on the other hand, I have learned to look carefully at everything I see and to consider its importance. This morning I saw the tracks of a camel that was lost. I knew he was lost because there were no human tracks near the tracks of the camel. I also noted that the camel must be blind in the right eye, because the grass on that side of the tracks was always left untouched while the grass on the left side was eaten. The animal was lame because with one foot he left a track so light that it could barely be seen. I also noted that he lacked one tooth because, wherever he ate grass, there was always a small space left untouched. I also found on the ground near the tracks of the camel groups of ants that were pulling grains of corn. I also found groups of flies that were busily eating drops of honey along the way. From these signs I was able to know the cargo that the animal was carrying."

COMPREHENSION AND CONVERSATION

1. Where was the Arab in the story walking?
2. Whom did the Arab meet? What had they lost?
3. What does *blind* mean? What is the meaning of *lame*? Do you know any blind or lame people?
4. What was wrong with the camel's mouth?

5. What cargo was the camel carrying?
6. What did the merchants think when the Arab told them that he had never seen their camel? Would you have believed him?
7. Where did they take him? What did they then claim?
8. How did the Arab know that the camel was lost? How did he know it was blind in one eye?
9. How did he know the camel was lame in one foot? How did he know what cargo the camel was carrying?
10. What is a desert? Name some of the most famous deserts in the world.
11. What is the difference between *desert* and *dessert?*
12. Why are camels used so frequently for carrying cargo in the desert?
13. Did the Arab in the story turn out to be a thief?
14. Do you think the camel in the story was young or old? Why?
15. A person who cannot see is called blind. What do we call a person who cannot hear? A person who cannot speak?

PRACTICE DRILL   Direct and Indirect Speech

The Arab said, "I *am* neither a thief nor a magician." The Arab said that he *was* neither a thief nor a magician. He said, "I *haven't seen* the camel." He said that he *hadn't seen* the camel. He said, "This morning I *saw* the tracks of a camel." He said that he *had seen* the tracks of a camel that morning. The Arab said, "I *don't know* where he is." The Arab said that he *didn't know* where he was.

John said, "I *am* too busy to leave." John said that he *was* too busy to leave. He said, "I *will be* back at two o'clock." He said that he *would be* back at two o'clock. Mary said, "I *can speak* English quite well now." Mary said that she *could speak* English quite well.

The merchants asked, "Where *is* the camel now?" The merchants asked where the camel *was* then. The merchants asked the Arab, "What *have* you *done* with the camel and the jewels?" The merchants asked the Arab what he *had done* with the camel and the jewels. The Arab asked, *"Is* the camel blind in one eye?" The Arab asked *whether* the camel *was* blind in one eye. The Arab asked, *"Has* he *lost* a tooth?" The Arab asked *whether* he *had lost* a tooth.

EXERCISE

Change these sentences from direct to indirect discourse, as in the example.

Example: *Jane said, "I don't know where my husband is."*
              (Jane said she didn't know where her husband was.)

1. The Arab asked the men, "Did you lose a camel?"
2. He said, "I haven't seen the camel."
3. She said, "I wish I had more cows."
4. We replied, "We want to go to the movies with you."
5. You answered, "I don't know where your keys are."
6. They promised, "We'll be back by two o'clock."
7. The teacher asked, "Can your friend speak English?"
8. The student answered, "I have done all my homework."

Change these sentences from indirect to direct discourse, as in the example.

Example: *He said he hadn't seen the camel.*
              (He said, "I haven't seen the camel.")

9. He said he was an excellent magician.
10. She told us she was too busy to help.
11. We asked whether the camel was lame.

12. We asked whether the camel had wandered off in the desert.
13. They said they wanted to visit their grandparents.
14. I replied that I wished I were in Florida.
15. You said you couldn't go with us.

VOCABULARY

Use each of these terms in a sentence:
to leave untouched, each other, along the way, Arab, desert, merchant, camel, blind, tooth, load, drop, honey, jewel, cargo, to accompany, to lead, to claim, thief, magician, tracks, human, to note, untouched, lame, hardly, grass, space, ant, grain.

REVIEW   The Passive Form

1. In what countries is Spanish spoken? In what countries is English spoken?
2. By whom was America discovered? In what year?
3. By whom is the mail delivered each day? How many times a day is it delivered?
4. In what kind of store are books sold? In what kind are men's suits and ties sold?
5. In what kind of store can a watch be bought? In what kind can fruit be bought?
6. Is your English class taught by a man or a woman? Was this book written by a man or a woman?
7. At what time of day can you be reached by telephone?
8. By whom are your English tests corrected?
9. Can English be learned in a year, or is more time necessary? How about other languages?
10. Can letters be mailed anywhere or only in certain places? Where are these places?

11. Where can stamps be bought?
12. When was the Declaration of Independence signed by representatives of the original thirteen colonies?
13. Is Independence Day in the United States celebrated on June fourth or on July fourth?
14. On what day of the year is Memorial Day observed?
15. Approximately how many new words have to be learned in each lesson of this book?

lesson (19)

At the Barbershop

"Good morning. Do I need an appointment?"

"No, sir, there's only one person ahead of you. You won't have to wait long."

"Thank you." (The customer takes a seat and looks through several magazines that are on the table.)

(Ten minutes later) "All right, sir, it's your turn. What will it be today?"

"I've been wearing my hair long for years, but now I'd like to try some kind of modern style. What do you suggest for a man like me, that is, with hair like mine?"

(The barber calls over a hair stylist, who shows the customer pictures of several different hair styles for men. The three of them confer, and they all agree on one style.)

"Come back here, please, sir. We'd like to wash your hair

94

first. That way it will be easier to cut and style. I think you'll like the style you've chosen. It's very fashionable."

"I hope so. I'm really tired of this old-fashioned cut that I've been wearing."

(The barber finishes cutting.) "Would you like me to blow-dry your hair? It will add fluff and lightness to the look."

"Yes, if you think it will help."

(The barber blow-dries the customer's hair and combs it. He then holds up a mirror so the customer can see both the front and the back.)

"What do you think of it?"

"It's great! Will it be hard to care for?"

"Not at all. When you wash it, it will fall into place naturally. You'll probably need another cut in about a month. Shall I make an appointment for you?"

"By all means."

COMPREHENSION AND CONVERSATION

1. Where does this conversation take place? Between what two people?
2. What does the customer think of his current hair style?
3. How does he pass the time while waiting for his turn?
4. What is a *hair stylist*? Have you ever been to one? What do hair stylists do?
5. When was the last time you had a haircut? Did you have your hair styled, too? What was it like?
6. How does the customer in the story decide on a hair style?
7. Why does the customer have his hair washed before he has it cut and styled?
8. Why does the barber want to blow-dry the customer's hair?
9. What does *blow-dry* mean? Do you ever blow-dry your hair or have your hair blow-dried?

10. How can a customer in a barbershop see his hair from all angles?
11. How did the customer react to his new hair style?
12. What did the barber tell him about his new cut?
13. What kind of hair do you have, wavy, curly, or straight?
14. Do you like to go to the barbershop? How much does it cost you to have your hair cut?
15. Do you wear your hair long or short? Do you have a part? Where?

PRACTICE DRILL   Causatives

The barber cuts John's hair every two weeks. John *has* his hair *cut* every two weeks (by the barber). I shine my shoes every day. I *have* my shoes *shined* every day. I repair my watch myself. I always *have* my watch *repaired* at Smith's Jewelry Store.

Mary *had* two teeth *pulled* yesterday. I am going to *have* my car *fixed* before I go away. He always *has* his shirts *made* especially for him. Helen *has* her nails *manicured* every week. She also *has* her hair *set* at the same time. We are going to *have* our house *painted* white. I must *have* my shoes *fixed*.

EXERCISE

Answer these questions using the appropriate causative form.
1. How often do you have your hair cut?
2. Where do you have your hair cut?
3. Do you ever have your shoes shined, or do you shine them yourself?
4. How much does it cost to have your shoes repaired?
5. Where do you send your clothes to have them cleaned?

6. How much does it cost today to have a man's suit dry-cleaned? A woman's suit?
7. How many times a year do you have your teeth cleaned by a dentist?
8. When was the last time you had a tooth pulled? A tooth filled?
9. When was the last time you had your house or apartment painted?
10. Have you ever had to have your watch repaired?

VOCABULARY

Use each of these terms in a sentence:
appointment, ahead of, to have to wait, to take a seat, to read through, to be someone's turn, What will it be?, haircut, style, to suggest, barber, barbershop, hair stylist, to confer, fashionable, old-fashioned, to blow-dry, fluff, lightness, mirror, to care for, to fall into place, by all means, current, wavy, curly, straight, part (in one's hair), angle.

REVIEW

1. What color hair do you have?
2. What do we mean when we say that a woman is a blonde? A brunette? A redhead?
3. What kind of material is a pencil made of? What is a chair made of? A window?
4. Of what kind of material are shoes made?
5. How much does a good pair of shoes cost today?
6. Which will last longer, a house made of wood or a house made of stone?
7. How much does a meal in a good restaurant cost?

8. Where does one go to have shoes repaired? To have them shined?
9. Where does one go to have clothes cleaned? To have them made?
10. Where does one go to have one's watch repaired? To have one's car repaired?
11. Is it expensive to have one's car repaired? To have one's teeth fixed?
12. What's the name of your family dentist? Your family doctor?
13. Where does one go to buy groceries? Newspapers? Books? Shoes?
14. What do you call a person who has no hair? Do you know anyone who has no hair?
15. If you had no hair, would you wear a wig? Why?

lesson 20

The Difficulties of a Foreign Language

One day, three international travelers were discussing the difficulties they had encountered while traveling in foreign countries. The stories they told all had to do with communicating in a foreign language when there were no interpreters present.

A young woman from France told of an incident while she was traveling in the United States.

"I was eating in a restaurant in Detroit," she said, "and I wanted to order some mushrooms. I was unable to make myself understood, so I asked for a pencil and paper and I carefully drew a picture of a mushroom."

"That sounds like a perfect solution," her companions said together.

"I thought so, too," she continued, "but my drawing was not

too good, because the puzzled waiter returned in about ten minutes, not with an order of mushrooms, but with a large umbrella!"

They all laughed. The German then told his story of a trip in Spain. He was, he said, unable to speak a word of Spanish.

"One day, while eating in a restaurant in a small village, I was having considerable difficulty explaining to the waiter that I wanted a glass of milk. Finally, I drew a picture of a cow on the back of the menu, and I indicated the appropriate gestures how to get the milk from the cow."

"What happened next?" his companions asked.

"The waiter still seemed puzzled. He looked at the picture for a very long time. Finally, he left and was gone from the restaurant for almost half an hour. When he returned at last, obviously pleased with what he had obtained, he handed me a ticket for a bullfight."

The Frenchwoman and the German turned to the Russian. "What's your story?" they asked.

"It doesn't have to do with a restaurant," he answered, "but rather with an English idiom. It's a short story, so I'll tell it quickly. It seems there is an idiom in English which means that when a person is not near you, you do not think of him or her. The idiom is, *out of sight, out of mind*. When I translated this into Russian in a class I was taking, I said it meant 'invisible idiot.' You can imagine how much laughter there was in the classroom! However, I learned a good idiom, and I passed my English course."

COMPREHENSION AND CONVERSATION

1. What are the nationalities of the people involved in this conversation?
2. What kinds of stories are they telling each other? Why?

3. Where was the Frenchwoman eating, and what did she want to order?
4. How did she try to communicate with the waiter? What were the results of her attempts?
5. Where was the German eating, and what did he want to communicate to his waiter?
6. What method of communication did he attempt? What were the results?
7. What is a bullfight? Where are bullfights usually held? Have you ever seen one?
8. What did the Russian's story have to do with?
9. How did he mistranslate the English idiom?
10. What is the actual meaning of *out of sight, out of mind?*
11. Have you traveled in any foreign countries? What languages were spoken in these countries?
12. Have you ever had any difficulties communicating in a foreign language in a restaurant or other place?
13. Do you think you are currently able to make yourself understood in English?
14. If you didn't know how to make yourself understood in a restaurant, what would you do?
15. What is an interpreter? A translator?

PRACTICE DRILL   Gerunds

They have stopped *studying* English. We enjoy *going* to the theater. Would you mind *waiting* for me a few minutes? I dislike *riding* on the subway. The man admitted *taking* the money. We would appreciate *hearing* from you at your earliest convenience. The driver of the car could not avoid *hitting* the child. They have finished *painting* the house. He did not deny *going* there. He could not risk *being seen* on the street. I didn't mind his *borrowing* my book, but I did mind his *keeping* it. He admitted *being* there on that night.

EXERCISE

Answer these questions in complete sentences, using gerunds wherever possible.
1. Which do you enjoy more, playing cards or playing baseball?
2. Which do you enjoy more, going to a movie or going to the theater?
3. Which do you enjoy more, walking in the country or walking along the city streets?
4. How many lessons have you finished studying in this book?
5. What language are you considering studying after you learn English?
6. Do you like traveling on trains? On planes?
7. Do you mind having to wait for people?
8. What sports do you enjoy playing? Watching? Talking about?
9. Do you enjoy writing to people in other countries?
10. Do you mind riding long distances in cars?

VOCABULARY

Use each of these terms in a sentence:
international, to encounter, to have to do with, interpreter, incident, mushroom, solution, companion, umbrella, a word of, village, considerable, to indicate, gesture, half an hour, obviously, bullfight, it seems, to translate, invisible, idiot, laughter, nationality, to be involved in, to communicate with, result, method, gerund, to borrow, convenience, subway.

REVIEW

1. If today were a holiday, where would you go?
2. If yesterday had been a holiday, where would you have gone?
3. If you were a millionaire, how would you spend your money? What is the first thing you would buy?
4. Are you able to draw well? Could you draw a mushroom or an umbrella?
5. Where do mushrooms grow? Do you like eating them?
6. When does one use an umbrella? Do you have one? What does it look like?
7. Do you like to drink milk? What kind of milk do you drink?
8. How does one get milk from a cow? Have you ever milked a cow?
9. If you were free to travel wherever you wanted, what places would you visit?
10. If friends were to come to visit you tonight, how would you entertain them?
11. If friends had come to visit you last night, how would you have entertained them?
12. If you can read English easily next year, what books will you read?
13. If you had been born in Italy, what language would you have learned as a child?
14. If you study hard, will you get a better mark on your next test?
15. If you had studied harder, would you have gotten a better mark on your last test?

A Telephone Conversation

"Good morning. Wilson Associates."

"This is Ms. Lopez speaking. I'd like to speak to Mr. Thomas, please."

"I'm sorry, but Mr. Thomas left the office a few minutes ago."

"That's too bad! I've been trying to call him for the last ten minutes, but your line has been busy. Will he be back soon?"

"I'm afraid not. He's gone for the rest of the day."

"Is there anywhere I can reach him?"

"I don't believe so. He's going out of town on business. Is there any message I can give him?"

"I had a business appointment with him for tomorrow morning at ten o'clock, but I'm afraid I can't make it."

"Would you care to make another appointment?"

"Unfortunately, I'm leaving town rather unexpectedly, and I may be gone for several days."

"I see. I can tell Mr. Thomas that you phoned."

"I wanted to speak to him before I left."

"If it is urgent, you might try phoning him at his home tonight."

"Yes, I might do that. What is his home telephone number, please?"

"His home number is 555-4758."

"I can reach him, I presume, around eight o'clock?"

"Possibly. I'm not sure what time you can reach him."

"In any case, thank you for your trouble. If I don't reach him at his home, you'll tell him, of course, that I called?"

"I certainly will. Good-bye."

COMPREHENSION AND CONVERSATION

1. Where does this conversation take place? Between what two people?
2. What has Ms. Lopez been trying to do for the last ten minutes?
3. What does it mean if a line is busy? What sound does the phone make when a line is busy?
4. Where does his secretary say Mr. Thomas is going?
5. Do you ever go out of town on business?
6. Why was Ms. Lopez calling?
7. Why can't she make another appointment?
8. What does the secretary suggest that Ms. Lopez do?
9. When is she going to try to call Mr. Thomas? Where? At what number?
10. What is your home number? When can you usually be reached by phone?
11. Why does Ms. Lopez thank the secretary?

12. Would you like to be a secretary? Do you enjoy answering the phone and taking messages?
13. Do you have any difficulty speaking English over the phone?
14. What is a long-distance call? A local call? A touch-tone phone?
15. How much does it cost to make a call from a pay phone in your area?

PRACTICE DRILL   Gerunds with Prepositions

John has difficulty *in learning* English. Helen is fond *of swimming*. William insisted *on postponing* the lesson. He has no intention *of returning* to the class. We are looking forward *to meeting* Helen's cousin. William has had little experience *in driving* a car. We are thinking *of going* to Canada on our vacation. We were prevented *from attending* the lecture by the bad weather. There is little possibility *of seeing* him today.

EXERCISE

Answer these questions using a preposition with a gerund.
1. Are you thinking of studying another language after you finish studying English?
2. Is there a chance of your visiting Europe next year?
3. Have you had much difficulty in mastering English pronunciation?
4. Do you have a problem with English vocabulary?
5. How long will a quartz watch run on one battery?
6. Have you had any experience in driving a truck?
7. Is there any possibility of our going to the rock concert tonight?

8. Where are you thinking of going on your next vacation?
9. Are you getting bored with studying English?
10. Are you looking forward to finishing this exercise?

VOCABULARY

Use each of these terms in a sentence:
to be too bad, to be back, rock concert, the rest of the day, to make an appointment, to be bored with, to wind (a watch), touch-tone, long-distance, to be reached, message, appointment, to care, unexpected, urgent, to presume, welcome, goodbye, secretary, intention, forward, to meet, cousin, to prevent, possibility, to dance, chance, to master, ordinary.

REVIEW

1. Do you have to make many phone calls each day? Do you receive many?
2. Is the telephone service usually good in your area?
3. What part of the telephone is the receiver?
4. What is an operator? What are an operator's duties?
5. What time is your lesson supposed to begin? To end?
6. In what room are we supposed to have our English class?
7. Which is supposed to be faster, the bus or the subway?
8. What time do you get up in the morning?
9. How long does it usually take you to get over a cold?
10. Do you get tired easily if you have to walk a long distance?

Fill in the blanks with *on* or *off*.

11. When I enter a room, I usually turn the light _____.
12. When I'm finished washing my hands, I turn the water _____.

13. When I want to watch TV, I turn it _____.
14. Before I go to bed at night, I turn the light _____.
15. When we want to listen to music, we turn the stereo _____.

lesson 22

Mark Twain as a Lecturer

In addition to being famous as a writer, Mark Twain was also famous in his day as a lecturer and a teller of funny stories. He frequently went from town to town giving lectures that included a series of funny stories.

One day, he was walking down the street of a small town where he was going to deliver a lecture that evening. A young man approached him and said, "Mr. Twain, I'd like to talk to you for a minute, please. I have an uncle that I'm very fond of. The problem is he never laughs or smiles. Is there anything you can suggest?"

"Bring your uncle to my lecture this evening, young man. I guarantee that he'll laugh and smile. Don't worry about a thing."

That evening the young man and his uncle sat in the first row.

Mark Twain spoke directly to them. He told some rather funny stories, but the old man never even smiled. Then he told the funniest stories in his repertoire, but the old man's face still remained blank. Mark Twain left the platform almost exhausted.

Later Mark Twain was telling a friend about the incident.

"Oh!" said the friend. "You could have saved yourself all your trouble. I know that old man. He has been deaf for years."

COMPREHENSION AND CONVERSATION

1. Who was Mark Twain? What was he famous for?
2. Why was he walking down the street of a small town?
3. Who approached him? What did the young man say?
4. What was Twain's suggestion for the young man?
5. Where did the young man and his uncle sit? Why?
6. How do you think Twain felt when the old man didn't laugh at his funny stories?
7. What did he discover later about the old man?
8. Did Twain live in the nineteenth or the twentieth century?
9. What are the names of some of the famous novels which Twain wrote?
10. Who is your favorite novelist? What are the names of some famous novelists in your country?
11. Do you know anyone who is deaf? How do deaf people communicate?
12. Have you ever attended a lecture where the lecturer told funny stories? Did you laugh? Did the audience laugh?
13. Do you know any funny stories? Tell one.
14. Have you ever given a lecture? Would you like to give one?
15. Do you enjoy attending lectures?

PRACTICE DRILL   Infinitives

We were pleased *to meet* him. We were pleased *to have met* him. I am glad *to meet* you. I am glad *to have met* you.

John seems *to learn* quickly. John seems *to be learning* quickly. He is supposed *to study* in this room every day. He is supposed *to be studying* in this room now.

They are supposed *to deliver* the books today. The books are supposed *to be delivered* tomorrow. The books were supposed *to have been delivered* yesterday.

The teacher made us *write* a composition for our homework. He also let us *go* home early. Will you help me *move* this dresser? No one heard him *knock* at the door. The servant saw him *leave* by the rear window. I like to watch the boys *play* tennis. I felt someone *touch* my elbow lightly. Mark Twain tried to make the old man *laugh*.

EXERCISE

Answer these questions in complete sentences using an infinitive.

1. Do you seem to be making good progress in English?
2. When you meet someone, do you say, "I'm pleased to meet you" or "I'm pleased to have met you"?
3. In which room are you supposed to have your class?
4. How many words are you supposed to learn today?
5. Does your teacher ever let you go home early from class?
6. What world-famous artists have you heard sing or play an instrument?
7. What sports do you enjoy watching people play?
8. What famous people have you heard speak on TV?
9. What did you have to write for homework last night?
10. How old were you when you learned to swim?

VOCABULARY

Use each of these terms in a sentence:
in addition, lecturer, series, one day, street, to deliver, to approach (someone), to be fond of, to laugh, to smile, to suggest, to guarantee, row, rather, repertoire, blank, platform, exhausted, to save oneself trouble, deaf, novelist, to attend, elbow, tennis, world-famous, instrument, infinitive, to make good progress, artist, to be pleased to.

REVIEW

1. Who is taller, you or your cousin?
2. Which is the largest city, New York, Chicago, or Washington, D.C.?
3. Which is the more expensive metal, gold or silver?
4. Do you wear a wrist watch? Of what metal is it made?
5. What time is it? What time will it be when this class ends?
6. How many clocks do you have at home? Do they run well?
7. Do your clocks ever gain or lose time? How do you fix them?
8. How often do you have to replace your watch battery?
9. What happens to a watch if you drop it?
10. Do you read a daily newspaper? Which one?
11. Which sections of the newspaper do you read on Sunday?
12. What magazines do you read regularly? Which is your favorite?
13. What magazines does your family subscribe to?
14. What was the last book you read? Who wrote it?
15. When was the last time you wrote a letter? To whom? Did the person write back?

lesson (23)

Seeing Someone Off

Three men stood drinking at a bar near a railroad station. They were waiting for a train and had, therefore, asked the porter to inform them when the train arrived. A short time later, the porter appeared in the doorway of the bar to tell them that the train was just coming in.

"Ah!" said the men. "We have time for just one more drink." They then all took another drink and ran out, but they missed the train.

They went back to the bar in order to await the arrival of the next train. They continued drinking. An hour later, the second train arrived, and the same thing happened. They missed the train again.

Two hours later, the porter appeared to say that the third and last train was just coming in. Again the men waited long enough to have one more drink, and then they all ran out. Two of the men, being tall, could run fairly fast. They caught the train. But the third man, who was short, again missed the train. Very slowly, he walked back to the bar and began drinking again.

"By the way," the bartender said to him after a while, "where are your two friends going?"

"I don't know where they're going," the man said. "They just came down to the station to see me off."

COMPREHENSION AND CONVERSATION

1. What were the three men doing at the railroad station?
2. How were they passing their time?
3. What arrangement did they have with the porter?
4. How did it happen that they missed the first train?
5. When did the second train come? What happened when it came?
6. How long a wait did the men have for the third and last train?
7. What did they do when the third train arrived?
8. Why did the third man miss the train? Where did he go after he missed it?
9. What conversation did he have with the bartender?
10. What is a bartender? What kind of work do bartenders do?
11. Have you ever missed a train? A plane? A bus? Explain the circumstances.
12. Do you like to travel by train? Would you ever like to work on a railroad?
13. What is the person who carries your bag at a railroad station or on a train called?
14. Who is the person who drives the train? The person who takes the passengers' tickets? The person who takes care of

the sleeping cars? What are some of the other people who work on a train called?

15. Do you know anyone who misses appointments frequently?

PRACTICE DRILL   Adjectives after Linking Verbs

Mary looked *cold*. This egg does not taste *fresh*. You seem very *uncomfortable* sitting there in that chair. The milk seemed very *sour* to me. The flowers smell *sweet*. Mr. Smith appears *weak* after his illness. You look very *strong* and *healthy* after your vacation. The air smells very *fresh* this morning. The room, though well furnished, did not look too *clean*. Helen seems exceedingly *happy* about something.

John looks *cold*. John looked at us *coldly*. He seems *angry*. He spoke to us *angrily*. She seems to be a very *sweet* person. She smiled at us *sweetly*. The man definitely looked *suspicious* to me. The police officer looked at the man very *suspiciously*. John feels *strong* again after his illness. John feels very *strongly* about certain political issues.

EXERCISE

Answer these questions in complete sentences using an adjective after the verb.

1. Do lemons taste sweet or sour?
2. Do flowers generally smell pleasant?
3. Do you ever feel angry toward your friends?
4. When a person is ill, does he or she generally feel strong or weak?
5. Does your classroom usually look clean?
6. When does the air smell fresher, in the morning or in the evening?

7. Do you feel tired today?
8. In what kind of weather do you feel most comfortable?
9. What kind of person does your next-door neighbor seem to be?
10. Late at night, do you usually look tired?

VOCABULARY

Use each of these terms in a sentence:
bar, railroad station, porter, to wait for, therefore, to inform, ah, doorway, to come in, to see someone off, to catch a train, to miss a train, to await, in order to, fairly, by the way, to pass one's time, arrangement, exceedingly, suspiciously, political, issue, police officer.

REVIEW

1. What is the opposite of the word *beautiful? Broad? Convenient?*
2. Which of the following is a synonym for the word *century:* the West Coast, a heavy cargo, a common disease, one hundred years?
3. Which of the following is a synonym for *boring:* alert, interesting, active, dull?
4. Which of the following is a food: beach, battle, brunette, basket, bacon?
5. Which of the following words is misspelled: beauty, complete, commerceal, comparison, continent?
6. What is the opposite of the word *comfortable?*
7. What is a common synonym for the word *expensive?*
8. What is your father's sister called?

9. Which of the following is used by a barber: a cot, clippers, an essay, a fable?
10. When you get on a bus, which of the following do you pay: a fee, a charge, a salary, a fare?
11. Animals sometimes live in which of the following: corners, caves, markets, jewelry shops?
12. What is the opposite of *noisy?*
13. On which of the following can you sleep: crowd, cargo, cot, dime?
14. Which of the following is used to make clothing: cheese, cotton, dessert, diplomacy?
15. Which of the following are you most likely to find in a bedroom: elbow, giraffe, idiom, dresser?

lesson (24)

A Clever Escape

A wise judge, who served in a district of England governed by an unjust man, was once condemned to prison in a tower because the governor was displeased by the great affection which the people felt for him. The tower was very high, and the judge was condemned to spend his entire life there all alone.

He had been in this prison for some time without hope of escape when one night, looking out of the window, he saw his wife standing at the foot of the tower. She was crying bitterly.

The judge called to her and said, "Don't cry, my dear, and listen carefully to what I am going to say. Go and bring back a scarab, a little butter, some silk thread, a heavy cord, and a rope. If you bring these things right away, I will possibly be able to escape from here."

His wife left and, within an hour, had returned with the things which her husband had asked her to bring. The judge said from above, "Put a little butter on the head of the scarab, tie the silk thread around its body, and place it on the wall with its head facing upwards."

The woman did all this very carefully. The scarab, which is very fond of butter, smelled the butter and thought that the butter was on the wall above. Thus it began to climb upwards.

The judge waited anxiously above for the scarab to reach him. When it came close, he picked it up and removed the thread from its body. To the lower end of the silk thread, his wife now tied the heavy cord, and to the end of the heavy cord, the piece of rope. The judge then pulled up the silk, then the cord, and finally the rope. He then tied the rope securely within the tower, and, going out through the window, slid down the rope until he reached the ground. There his wife awaited him, not only pleased that he had escaped but greatly surprised that a poor scarab had served to carry out a task so important.

COMPREHENSION AND CONVERSATION

1. With whom is this story concerned?
2. Why was the judge condemned to prison?
3. For how long was he condemned?
4. What was his wife doing when he saw her from his window? Why was she doing this?
5. What instructions did he give her?
6. What did she do with the butter and the scarab? What is a scarab?
7. Why did the scarab climb upwards?
8. What did the judge do when the scarab reached him?
9. Do you know anyone in prison? Why are people sent to prison?
10. What do you think of the judge's method of escaping from prison?

11. What are the duties of a judge?
12. Do you think you'd like to be a judge? Why?
13. What is a tower? Why do you think people build towers?
14. What is thread used for? What is rope used for? What is cord used for?
15. Of all the items used by the judge and his wife in the escape, which do you think was the most important?

PRACTICE DRILL   Special Verbs: *lie, lay; rise, raise; sit, set*

The men will come to *lay* the rug today. Mary *has laid* all her books on my desk. John *laid* the newspaper on the chair. John was very tired and *lay* down for an hour. I think I will *lie* down and rest for an hour. The dog *has been lying* in that position all afternoon.

Will you please *raise* the window? It was dark in the room, so I asked him to *raise* the curtain. What time will the sun *rise* tomorrow? Mary *rose* to her feet suddenly and left the room.

John will *sit* in this seat during the lesson today. We *sat* in the sun for two hours. You can *set* those flowers on Mr. Smith's desk. When we arrived, Mary had already *set* the table.

EXERCISE

Answer these questions using the correct verb form.
1. Do you ever lie down to rest in the afternoon?
2. Do you always hang up your hat and coat when you arrive home, or do you sometimes lay them on a chair?
3. Does the sun always rise at the same time, or does the time vary according to the season?
4. What time did the sun rise yesterday?
5. What time does the sun rise during the present season?

6. What time will the sun set today?
7. What time did the sun set yesterday?
8. Does the sun always set at the same time, or does the time vary according to the season?
9. Do you find the sunset a pleasant time of the day?
10. When was the last time you saw the sun rise?
11. If a room is too warm, do you raise or close the window?
12. If a room is too dark, do you raise or lower the curtain?
13. Do you always put your books away when you finish studying, or do you generally let them lie around the room?
14. Do you like to lie in the sun at the beach?
15. What sometimes happens if a person lies in the sun too long?

VOCABULARY

Use each of these terms in a sentence:
judge, district, governor, to condemn, prison, tower, affection, foot, scarab, silk, thread, cord, rope, upwards, anxious, secure, to slide, task, all alone, right away, to carry out, for some time, in an hour, at the foot (top) of, brother-in-law, rug.

REVIEW

1. What is the opposite of *late?* Of *remember?* Of *honest?*
2. Which of the following people takes care of your teeth: a doctor, a dentist, a judge, a bus driver?
3. Which of the following is a synonym for *lately:* recently, behind time, modern, long ago?
4. Which of the following is a food: license, lecture, risk, mushroom?

5. Which of the following words is misspelled: misplace, miracle, manicure, mathametics?
6. What is the opposite of the word *near?*
7. What is your wife's mother called?
8. Which of the following is used in a restaurant: repertoire, radio, menu, novel?
9. What do you use a *timetable* for?
10. What is a common synonym for the word *rapid?*
11. Which of the following would you be most likely to use in bad weather: railroad, synonym, skates, raincoat?
12. What is the opposite of *loose?*
13. Which of the following is often very sour: storm, lemon, stone, sugar?
14. Which of the following is used to make clothing: silk, sunlight, soil, toast?
15. Which of the following would you want if you were thirsty: rice, tickets, tobacco, water?

APPENDIX

Principal Parts of Common Irregular Verbs

Present	Past	Past Participle	Present	Past	Past Participle
arise	arose	arisen	eat	ate	eaten
awake	awoke	awakened	fall	fell	fallen
bear	bore	born	feed	fed	fed
bear	bore	borne	feel	felt	felt
beat	beat	beaten	fight	fought	fought
become	became	become	find	found	found
begin	began	begun	fling	flung	flung
bend	bent	bent	fly	flew	flown
bet	bet	bet	forget	forgot	forgotten
bind	bound	bound	forgive	forgave	forgiven
bite	bit	bitten	freeze	froze	frozen
bleed	bled	bled	get	got	gotten
blow	blew	blown	give	gave	given
bring	brought	brought	go	went	gone
build	built	built	grind	ground	ground
burst	burst	burst	grow	grew	grown
cast	cast	cast	hang	hung	hung
catch	caught	caught	have	had	had
choose	chose	chosen	hear	heard	heard
cling	clung	clung	hide	hid	hidden
come	came	come	hit	hit	hit
cost	cost	cost	hold	held	held
creep	crept	crept	hurt	hurt	hurt
cut	cut	cut	keep	kept	kept
dare	dared	dared	know	knew	known
deal	dealt	dealt	lay	laid	laid
dig	dug	dug	lead	led	led
do	did	done	leave	left	left
draw	drew	drawn	lend	lent	lent
drink	drank	drunk	let	let	let
drive	drove	driven	lie	lay	lain

Principal Parts of Common Irregular Verbs—*Continued*

Present	Past	Past Participle	Present	Past	Past Participle
light	lit	lit	speed	sped	sped
lose	lost	lost	spend	spent	spent
make	made	made	spin	spun	spun
mean	meant	meant	split	split	split
meet	met	met	spread	spread	spread
owe	owed	owed	spring	sprang	sprung
pay	paid	paid	stand	stood	stood
quit	quit	quit	steal	stole	stolen
read	read	read	stick	stuck	stuck
ride	rode	ridden	sting	stung	stung
ring	rang	rung	strike	struck	struck
rise	rose	risen	string	strung	strung
run	ran	run	swear	swore	sworn
see	saw	seen	sweep	swept	swept
seek	sought	sought	swim	swam	swum
sell	sold	sold	swing	swung	swung
send	sent	sent	take	took	taken
set	set	set	teach	taught	taught
shake	shook	shaken	tear	tore	torn
shave	shaved	shaved	tell	told	told
shine	shone	shone	think	thought	thought
shoot	shot	shot	throw	threw	thrown
show	showed	shown	wake	woke	woke
shrink	shrank	shrunk	wear	wore	worn
shut	shut	shut	weave	wove	woven
sing	sang	sung	wed	wed	wed
sink	sank	sunk	weep	wept	wept
sit	sat	sat	wet	wet	wet
sleep	slept	slept	win	won	won
slide	slid	slid	wind	wound	wound
slit	slit	slit	wring	wrung	wrung
speak	spoke	spoken	write	wrote	written

Sample Conjugations

Verb: *to be*

Present Tense

I am	we are
you are	you are
he, she, it is	they are

Present Perfect Tense

I have been	we have been
you have been	you have been
he has been	they have been

Past Tense

I was	we were
you were	you were
he was	they were

Past Perfect Tense

I had been	we had been
you had been	you had been
he had been	they had been

Future Tense

I will be	we will be
you will be	you will be
he will be	they will be

Verb: *to work* (simple form)

Present Tense

I work	we work
you work	you work
he, she, it works	they work

Present Perfect Tense

I have worked	we have worked
you have worked	you have worked
he has worked	they have worked

Past Tense

I worked	we worked
you worked	you worked
he worked	they worked

Past Perfect Tense

I had worked	we had worked
you had worked	you had worked
he had worked	they had worked

Future Tense

I will work	we will work
you will work	you will work
he will work	they will work

Sample Conjugations—*Continued*

Verb: *to work* (continuous form)

Present Tense

I am working   we are working

you are working   you are working

he, she, it is working   they are working

Past Tense

I was working   we were working

you were working   you were working

he was working   they were working

Future Tense

I will be working   we will be working

you will be working   you will be working

he will be working   they will be working

Present Perfect Tense

I have been working   we have been working

you have been working   you have been working

he has been working   they have been working

Past Perfect Tense

I had been working   we had been working

you had been working   you had been working

he had been working   they had been working

Consonants

[p]—pie, hope, happy

[b]—bell, bite, globe

[f]—fine, office

[v]—vest, of, have

[k]—keep, can, book

[g]—go, get, egg

[l]—let, little, lay

[m]—man, must, dime

[n]—no, down, ton

[ŋ]—sing, ringing

[w]—water, we, one

[θ]—thin, three, path

[ð]—they, then, other

[s]—see, sat, city

[z]—zoo, does, is

[ʃ]—shoe, ship, action

[ʒ]—usual, garage

[tʃ]—chance, watch

[dʒ]—June, edge

[r]—red, rich, write

[y]—you, yes, million

[h]—he, hat, who

[t]—ten, to, meet

[d]—do, did

Vowels and Diphthongs

[ɪ]—it, did, build

[i]—me, see, people

[ɛ]—end, let, any

[æ]—cat, bat, laugh

[ɑ]—army, father, hot

[ɔ]—all, caught, long

[ʊ]—book, full, took

[u]—too, move, fruit

[ə]—cup, soda, infant

[ɚ]—her, work, bird

[e]—say, they, mail

[o]—old, coal, sew

[aɪ]—dry, eye, buy

[ɔɪ]—toy, boy, soil

[aʊ]—cow, our, house

---

* *In accordance with common practice and for reasons of simplification, these minor changes in symbols have been introduced. [ə] and [ɚ] are used in this book for both stressed and unstressed syllables. [y] is used instead of IPA [j]. [ɑ] is used instead of IPA [a].*

NOTES

NOTES

NOTES

NOTES

NOTES